The Winnipeg General S

J. E. Rea

Canadian History Through the Press Series

General Editors:
David P. Gagan, Anthony W. Rasporich

Holt, Rinehart and Winston of Canada, Limited
Toronto : Montreal
Distributed in the United States of America by Winston Press,
Minneapolis

For L. K. and Z.

J. E. Rea is Associate Professor of History at the University of Manitoba,
Winnipeg.

Anthony W. Rasporich, general editor of the *Canadian History Through
the Press Series*, is currently Associate Professor of History at the University of Calgary, Alberta.

David P. Gagan, general editor of the *Canadian History Through the
Press Series*, is Assistant Professor of History at McMaster University,
Hamilton, Ontario.

Editors' Preface

Newspapers are widely accepted by historians as useful vehicles of contemporary opinion. In a nation such as Canada, historically dependent on books and periodicals imported from Great Britain and the United States as the principal disseminators of informed opinion, the local daily or weekly newspaper has been almost the sole native medium of information and attitudes. And the proliferation of Canadian newspapers since the early decades of the nineteenth century has created for students of Canadian history a vast reservoir of opinion reflecting the political, social, cultural, linguistic, religious and sectional diversity of our country. The *Canadian History Through the Press* series is an attempt to tap this reservoir by reproducing a cross section of journalistic opinion on major issues, events and problems of the Canadian past.

Using the press as a vehicle for the study of history has already been done with some success in the French series, *Kiosk*, which examines public issues and popular culture in volumes ranging from the Dreyfus affair to French cinéma. *Canadian History Through the Press* is not quite so ambitious a venture; but it does aim to introduce the student to events which were compelling subjects of discussion for Canadians through the medium in which public discussion most frequently took place. At its best, the Canadian press is a rich source of historical controversy, providing the historian with a sense of the excitement and contentiousness of contemporary issues. Newspaper editors like William Lyon Mackenzie, George Brown, Henri Bourassa and George McCullagh were themselves often at the centre of the political stage or were, like J. W. Dafoe of the Winnipeg *Free Press*, Joseph Atkinson of the Toronto *Star* and Gérard Pelletier of *La Presse* pundits whose voices were carefully heeded by national and local politicians. This is merely one example of the power of the press; but whatever the subject — Confederation, the Quiet Revolution, social reform, foreign policy or pollution — the press has operated (in Marshall McLuhan's words) as a "corporate or collective image [that] demands deep participation."

As editors of *Canadian History Through the Press* we are committed to the idea that students should be introduced to the study of Canadian history through contemporary documents from the very outset. The newspaper is a familiar, and therefore comfortable medium for the novice historian. We have chosen to use it exclusively, fully aware of the limitations of the press as an historical source. When a prominent Canadian politician observed recently that his colleagues spent much of their time "quoting yesterday's newspaper" he was acknowledging the power of the press not merely to reflect, but to dictate opinion. And Will Rogers' caricature of the man who "only knew what he read in the paper" is an equally cogent reminder that newspapers should not be used exclusively as a weathercock of opinion. The student, then, must and inevitably will come to grips with both the limitations and the advantages of newspapers as sources of history. In this respect, our series is also aimed at introducing the student to one of the historians most crucial problems, that of discriminating between conflicting accounts and interpretations of historical events.

The volumes currently planned for the *Canadian History Through the Press* series embrace topics ranging from the War of 1812 to the Quiet Revolution of the 1960's, from economic history to religious issues. While it is not immediately possible, we hope that in time the series will eventually embrace an even wider spectrum of subjects which permit us to sample not merely the thrust, but the quality, of Canadian life.

David P. Gagan,
Anthony W. Rasporich,
May, 1972.

Author's Preface

The Winnipeg General Strike has usually been considered something of an aberration in Canadian development, a brief, irrational dislocation resulting from four years of wartime emotion. Our country, on the whole, has not been plagued by massive confrontations of workers and the community. But it would be foolish to assume that we are able to consider ourselves removed from the social and economic implications of modern, industrial society, so productive of widespread alienation as well as material bounty.

Winnipeg's summer of apprehension in 1919 now merits only a paragraph or two in history textbooks. But in the life of the city it was a touchstone from which ramified its future political course. Its effect continues to condition our politics more than fifty years later. Students can still profitably consider the implications of such a dramatic rupture in the life of a community.

The newspaper sources on which this study is based are manifold. I have attempted to select those which best illustrate both the substantive issues involved in the Strike and the emotional reaction which they precipitated.

One incurs many obligations in the course of research which are impossible to acknowledge. But I would like, particularly, to thank Mr. Jay Atherton of the Public Archives of Canada; my colleague Dr. Lovell C. Clark of the University of Manitoba; Miss Blanche Miller for her patient and efficient typing and finally, Dr. David Gagan, an understanding and perceptive editor.

J. E. Rea,
Winnipeg.

Contents

Introduction

I

The Winnipeg General Strike began at 11 a.m. on May 15, 1919. It lasted six weeks less a day and concluded in riot, bloodshed, and the arrest of the strike leaders on charges of seditious conspiracy. The workers, in defence of their actions, explained that they were furthering the cause of working men not only in Winnipeg but the world over, that they were part of an international movement which must succeed, in time, in establishing a workers' Utopia. Their opponents, on the other hand, assumed that they were defending constituted authority against overthrow and replacement by an alien system of economic and political organization. Such apocalyptic interpretations of the events that took place in Winnipeg in the late spring of 1919 seem incredible, in retrospect. But the times, and the issues involved, as the newspaper commentary on the strike makes clear, combined to create the appearance that the tide of Bolshevism had been stemmed in the streets of Winnipeg, Manitoba.

Indeed, the hysteria was not at all localized for North America in 1919 was in the grip of the great "Red Scare." There was a widespread conviction in both Canada and the United States that the Russian Revolution had been packaged for export, that its harbingers were anarchism and industrial violence, and that Lenin and Trotsky, seeking new worlds to conquer, had settled on Winnipeg and Seattle as starting points. A similar general strike in Seattle in February, 1919 had been forcibly crushed, making Mayor Ole Hanson an unlikely national hero. There was no direct connection between the Seattle and Winnipeg Strikes, despite the rumours and allegations to the contrary.

> In the United States, the Winnipeg incident was reported in a most sensational manner. Eight-column headlines announced to a shocked public the events taking place there, and wide circulation was given exaggerated Canadian press releases. . . .[1]

So little was known of recent events in Russia – good or bad – that no story was too incredible for hopeful or apprehensive North Americans.

This was the climate of opinion in which the Winnipeg General Strike took place. Yet it came as almost a complete surprise to Canadians living east of the Lakehead. Quebec was preoccupied, licking its wounds from the conscription struggle. Most English-speaking Canadians in the east (and much of the rural west) saw the Great War as the crucible in which Canada's mature nationality was forged. There was not nearly as much enthusiasm for the war among the working men of western Canada, especially in Manitoba, British Columbia, and the mining district of Alberta.

Even before the armistice of November, 1918, restlessness in the ranks of western labour was turning to radicalism. *The Voice*, the Winnipeg-based labour newspaper edited by the moderate A. W. Puttee until it collapsed in July, 1918, reflected the discontent. Conscription, press censorship, war-profiteering were all cited as causes of the growing estrangement of western workers. But beyond all these, economic conditions and collective bargaining rights were the hard issues which were leading Winnipeg labour into new directions.

The cost of living increased sharply during the war without any corresponding improvement in real wages.[2] The more advanced element of Winnipeg labour blamed this on capitalist greed taking hypocritical advantage of patriotic zeal and the call for national sacrifice. It was felt as well that labour's legitimate right to organize and bargain collectively was being denied. Twice, just before the end of the war, these two issues provoked serious strikes in the city.

In May, 1918, most civic employees in Winnipeg went out in protest demanding wage increases. The city's services were badly crippled as employees in hydro, the waterworks, and the fire department were joined by electricians, teamsters, and the provincially-employed telephone operators. The strike assumed major proportions when four thousand railway workers left their jobs. For over three weeks sporadic negotiations continued and the Winnipeg Trades and Labour Council inconclusively discussed the calling of a general sympathy strike.

The tension was heightened when a conciliatory report by a negotiating committee appointed by City Council was almost swept aside by a new issue. Alderman Frank Fowler had introduced a motion denying to all civic employees the right to strike. It narrowly passed Council. The Fowler amendment effectively blocked any settlement. At this point, the Federal Minister of Labour, Gideon Robertson, a former craft unionist, intervened. He was successful in persuading City Council to abandon the amendment. Robertson's timely arrival was given added effect by the actions of the Committee of One Hundred. This Committee, composed of business and professional men and claiming to represent the public interest, had negotiated directly with the strikers and resolved all the outstanding difficulties. With the Fowler Amendment withdrawn the way was now open for a settlement. Labour was jubilant. Wage increases had been won and the right to strike conceded. Not enough importance, however, was attached by Labour to the aid given the civic employees by Robertson and the community.

Again in July, 1918, Winnipeg was distracted by a serious strike, this time among the metal workers. Members of the various metal trades were in the vanguard of the growing labour militancy in the city. Most of them worked in the railway shops, but many were employed in independent contract shops, the three largest of which were the Vulcan Iron Works, Manitoba Bridge and Iron Works, and the Dominion Bridge Company. The various metal trades were organized into a Metal Trades Council which claimed to represent all metal workers in the city. The managers of the contract shops refused to recognize the Metal Trades Council as a bargaining unit since, they argued, the Council was primarily an organization of employees of the railroad shops. Consequently, the contract shop managers ignored a new schedule of wages presented by the Metal Trades Council on June 1. After fruitless attempts at negotiation the metal workers struck on July 22. The three large contract shops applied for and received an injunction against picketing. In response, the metal workers sought the support of the Trades and Labour Council to which they were affiliated. The Council, in turn, polled its member unions on the question of a general strike in sympathy with the metal workers. The result was a seven to one affirmative vote.[3] Meanwhile, the contract shops had separately come to agreement with their own workmen and the threat of a general strike passed. The vital issue of recognition of the Metal Trades Council had not been resolved, merely evaded, for the moment.

For several reasons, the implications of the labour disputes of 1918 should not be underestimated when considering the background of the general strike of the following year. It is worth noting, initially, that the restraints of war did not dissuade Winnipeg workers from resorting to strike action to express their discontent. To see the events of 1919 as the release of pent up resentment held in check by the war is to misread the implications of the 1918 strikes and their witness to a new militancy in Winnipeg labour. On both occasions there was talk of a general strike and during the metal trades dispute there was a substantial expression of support in response to the call of the Trades and Labour Council.

The apparent willingness of Winnipeg workers to resort to the general strike as a tactical weapon revealed the new mood of western labour and the influence of more radical leaders. There was an obvious impatience with traditional craft union methods and attitudes. This new spirit was given expression by a rather remarkable set of men who came to prominence in Winnipeg labour circles in 1918 and 1919. There must have been several dozen who shared their views but the most important were George Armstrong, William Ivens, John Queen, R. J. (Dick) Johns, and R. B. (Bob) Russell. All of them came from Great Britain shortly before the war, except Armstrong who was born in Ontario. All of them were socialists of one stripe or another. And all of them were imbued with the more advanced ideas of British labour circles.

In particular, they were not satisfied with the conservative, business unionism which seemed to dominate North American labour. They were familiar with syndicalism but may be more closely identified with industrial unionism. This is a term that must be handled with care. It did not mean what it does now, simply collective bargaining within a whole industry. It is unlikely that the new leaders of Winnipeg labour would acknowledge a common intellectual source. They were hardly a homogeneous group. Yet, it seems clear that except for John Queen they could all accept the definition of industrial unionism associated with James Connolly, the Irish labour leader. The path for labour to follow, according to Connolly, was to create "an industrial republic inside the shell of the political State. . . ."[4] Once economic power was achieved, political power would follow willy-nilly.

This is not to suggest that Winnipeg labour leaders had anything quite so precise in mind. What is evident, however, is their conviction that labour's strength could only be marshalled effectively by going beyond the traditional craft organizations. Some method must be found to bring the workers together in larger groups in order to exert more strength. Within this context, the lessons of 1918 in Winnipeg become more apparent. For better or worse, the success of the civic employees' strike was attributed to the threat of a general strike – the exercise of the collective strength of Winnipeg's workers. It is hard to resist the interpretation that Russell and Johns, especially, were left a little giddy by it all. They were more than ever convinced that the effective consolidation of labour would open the door to opportunity.

How divergent the paths of eastern and western labour had become was dramatically demonstrated at the meeting of the Trades and Labour

Congress of Canada in September, 1918 in Quebec City. The westerners, among whom Russell was prominent, presented a crucial resolution which urged the convention to abandon craft unionism and move toward industrial organization. When it was resoundingly defeated, along with other resolutions submitted by Trades and Labour Councils in the west, the disenchantment was complete. The more radical western delegates returned home committed to the calling of a western labour convention that would strike out on its own.

Over the winter of 1918-19, the radicals, led by Russell, Johns, and Armstrong became increasingly influential in the Winnipeg Trades and Labour Council. They were never in a commanding position but a virtual balance was reached between them and the more moderate members. In addition, they were given vigorous support by the *Western Labor News*, edited by William Ivens, which had replaced the moderate labour newspaper *The Voice* in the summer of 1918. Neither radicals nor moderates were able to establish undisputed control in the Council but the latter seemed more and more on the defensive.

The direction in which the tide was running became much clearer in March, 1919 when the western labour movement convened in Calgary. Winnipeg sent forty-seven representatives, the largest delegation at the convention. If names were any indication, every one was of British origin and none of the leading Winnipeg moderate trade unionists were included. Russell was one of the dominant personalities of the meeting and Johns was chairman of the policy committee.

The most important result of the Calgary Convention was to approve the creation of the One Big Union.[5] The One Big Union was the institutional expression of the demand for industrial organization. The convention considered craft unionism a thing of the past. The One Big Union was based on the geographic (that is, provincial) organization of all workers, skilled and unskilled into one working class movement. Their new political and economic strength could then be deployed to accomplish the objectives of the working class. Equally important, in the aftermath of the convention, was the rhetoric which accompanied the various resolutions. There was a good deal of simplistic and rather primitive Marxism bandied about. The convention demanded the release of all political prisoners and sent fraternal greetings to the new Soviet government of Russia. Without a dissenting vote, the delegates enthusiastically endorsed "the principle of Proletarian Dictatorship as being absolute and efficient for the transformation of capitalist private property to communal wealth." In addition, there was widespread support for the calling of a general strike throughout the west on June 1 to give effect to the demands of the convention.[6]

It was an exhilarated band of delegates who returned to Winnipeg in early April. They had caught a vision of Utopia and the One Big Union was the vehicle to attain it. Rather naively, they saw the world divided into two groups, the workers and the bosses. There was no place in their thinking for the community as a whole with its rights. There was, however, an inexorable logic about another aspect of their thinking. If the One Big Union was designed to serve the needs and aspirations of the working class as a whole, then its technique must involve the mobilization of all the workers; thus, the almost casual resort to labour's ultimate and tragic weapon, the general strike. There does not appear to have been any clear conception of the impact of such a wholesale withdrawal of labour's services from the community.

The leaders of Winnipeg labour seem to have considered it simply a bigger and better strike in the traditional sense. It is important to recognize that moderate labour elements shared this view. The general strike was not an imposition of the radical leadership, but a method accepted by the mass of Winnipeg workers after the heady days of the spring and summer of 1918. Yet, in its essence, a general strike is something quite different from an ordinary strike which is the last step in the collective bargaining process. A general strike is an attempt to effect a massive and permanent shift in economic power from capital to labour. Once labour has attained this economic power, political power must follow. In a capitalist society based on middle class values, there were only two possible outcomes of such a drastic step. Either the strike would be broken or the workers would eventually take over. None of this was clear, however, in the exciting days of May, 1919 just before the general strike.

Events moved swiftly after Russell, Johns, and their colleagues returned from Calgary. Through the *Western Labor News* they preached the gospel of the One Big Union. The workers of Winnipeg were both receptive and restless. On May 1, the men in the building trades went out on strike after failing to win a new wage schedule from the Winnipeg Builders' Exchange. The following day the metal workers struck the contract shops for better wages and the inflammatory issue (at least to the employers) of recognition of the Metal Trades Council as bargaining agent. Both groups of strikers appealed to the Trades and Labour Council for support. After a highly emotional meeting, the

Council agreed to take a poll of all its member unions on the question of a general strike.

Over seventy affiliated unions took strike votes. The result was an overwhelming endorsation, over eleven thousand votes in favour and five hundred opposed. In the interval, both Mayor Charles F. Gray and Premier T. C. Norris had made last minute attempts to bring about a settlement in the building and metal trades without success. On Tuesday night, May 13, the Trades and Labour Council called a general strike to begin at 11 a.m., May 15.

II

It was a glorious spring in Winnipeg that year with warm and sunny days succeeding each other. It matched the mood of the men as they streamed from factories, plants and shops on Thursday morning. A picnic atmosphere prevailed and few thought the work stoppage would last long. The bosses would soon be brought to heel.

There have been various estimates of the number of men who joined the strike, but it is reasonably certain that about twenty-five thousand of Winnipeg's working force participated. The city was virtually paralysed within two or three days. Streetcar employees, firemen, railway shopmen, civic employees in all the utilities, postal workers, and practically all the smaller unions associated with the Trades and Labour Council responded to the call for a general strike. The three daily newspapers were shut down, telephone and telegraph services ended, movie houses and restaurants closed. The daily deliveries of bread, milk, and ice ceased. Water pressure was held so low that none reached higher than the second floor, a nice bit of planning since no working man could afford premises above that level. The police force had voted to strike as well, but remained on duty at the request of the strike committee. Winnipeg was isolated from the outside world and its citizens waited expectantly or apprehensively.

In the first flush of enthusiasm there was much half-facetious, half-serious rhetoric. William Ivens, the editor of the *Western Labor News* which published a daily *Strike Bulletin*, announced that a soviet had been set up in Winnipeg. It was suggested, as well, that the Manitoba Legislative building would make a grand labour temple. Even Ernest Robinson the moderate trade unionist and secretary of the Trades and Labour Council was carried away. "We have withdrawn labour from all industry," he told a Strikers Meeting on May 18, "and it will stay withdrawn until the bosses realize that they cannot stand against the masses of labour. If we can control industrial production now, at this time, we can control it for all time to come, and we can control the Government of this country, too."[7]

The leaders of the Strike Committee could muse over Robinson's words for other reasons. The complete withdrawal of labour places a community on the brink of chaos. Something must be done to maintain essential services or society will collapse. The police were in an obviously anomalous situation. They remained at their duty at the request of the Strike Committee but for how long they would continue to do so was problematical. Could the community depend on them to preserve order and protect property when their sympathies lay with the strikers? Even more immediate was the question of bread and milk deliveries. The families of the strikers were being put to the same inconvenience as the rest of the community. Infants and invalids knew no class lines. So the Strike Committee agreed to the resumption of deliveries on the 19th of May. In order to protect the drivers from charges of scabbing or physical violence (and, incidentally, to protect the property of the dairies and bakeries) the wagons carried signs which read "Permitted by authority of the Strike Committee." It was a common sense decision but it provoked a storm of criticism from the public. Not unnaturally, many nonparticipants began to ask the basic question of who was running the city, the elected government or the Strike Committee? The meaning of a general strike was becoming much more clear.

The first reaction of the business and professional class and many of those citizens who had no direct involvement in the strike was to organize in defence of the community. The Committee of One Hundred which had functioned in 1918 was revived and expanded into the Committee of One Thousand, or as it was more commonly known, the Citizens' Committee. Its primary aim was the restoration of essential services, especially fire protection and telephones. The Citizens' Committee proclaimed itself impartial in the original disputes in the building and metal trades. They were, however, stoutly opposed to the general strike, and since they were organized to maintain essential services, they were bound to collide with the Strike Committee which was denying those services to the city. The Citizens' Committee, in other words, was dedicated to breaking the general strike.

As the first shock of the strike ebbed the divided community began to take stock. The towers of capitalism had not toppled at the first blast of labour's trumpet, and the heady rhetoric of the first days of the strike was quickly muted. The *Western Labor News* now repeated daily that the only issues in the strike were collective bargaining and the right to a living wage. But the Citizens' Committee, in that year of the Red Scare, was convinced that Winnipeg was beset by a Bolshevist conspiracy. This led them, and their newspaper, *The Winnipeg Citizen*, into a tortured argument. A general strike was an alien doctrine, foreign to Canada, and subversive of British institutions. It became incumbent upon them to identify the Winnipeg strike with the aliens in defiance of the fact that all the strike leaders were English or Canadian and steeped in British trade unionist ideas. The Citizens hammered away at this alien theme and were supported by the Winnipeg dailies when they resumed publication.

The question of how seriously to take this rhetoric is one of the most difficult interpretive problems of the Winnipeg general strike. There has been a tendency to allow the extremist rhetoric of the Citizens' Committee to characterize that group and yet to dismiss the almost equally inflammatory statements of labour radicals as romantic idealism. This is somewhat illogical. Furthermore, in the polyglot population of Winnipeg, the long term effect of the rhetoric has been almost as profound as the reality of the issues of the strike.

In any case, after the strike had lasted a week the city was divided into two hostile and suspicious camps. Despite the apprehensions of many there had been no violence. Indeed, the absence of incident of any kind was remarkable. This was the result of the conscious policy of the Strike Committee. They knew full well that any disturbances would probably bring martial law and the breaking of the strike by force. The *Western Labor News* urged the strikers to stay off the streets, stay home, do nothing. It became almost a campaign of passive resistance.

But Winnipeg would not long remain in a state of suspended animation. Newspapers across the country were demanding intervention by the federal authorities. The Dominion Government was almost obliged to take a hand. The postal workers were federal employees and they had struck in violation of a valid collective agreement. It was the duty of the government to ensure the delivery of the mails. On May 24, an ultimatum was issued to the postal employees that they must return to work by noon of May 26 or be dismissed permanently from the civil service. With Prime Minister Robert Borden off at the Versailles Peace Conference, the actions of the federal government were directed by Arthur Meighen, the acting Minister of Justice, and Senator Gideon Robertson, the Minister of Labour. They would, in the end, be the effective agents in breaking the strike.

The civic authorities also took a direct role in the situation after almost two weeks of vacillation. City Council declared the sympathy strike illegal and all civic employees were discharged summarily. The situation further deteriorated when sympathetic strikes took place all across the west and Toronto was threatened by a massive general walkout. At this point the policy of the federal government became very clear. Senator Robertson telegraphed the Mayor of Calgary, whose city was hit by a sympathy strike, that the One Big Union sought to control civic, provincial, and federal governments and to subvert all constituted authority. Throughout the length of the strike, Robertson and Meighen clearly saw the One Big Union as the vanguard of revolution that had to be stopped.[8]

The situation in Winnipeg was further complicated by the presence of a potentially volatile element, the unemployed veterans of the Great War. Many of them had been trade unionists before the war and their sympathies naturally went out to labour. At the same time, they were on the whole deeply prejudiced against the central European portion of Winnipeg's population. Many were embittered by unemployment when the "aliens" held jobs. There is simply no way of determining how they divided in opinion. Veterans staged parades both for and against the strike. They were appealed to for support by both labour and the Citizens' Committee. The latter basely pandered to ethnic prejudice, thus inflicting even deeper wounds on the distracted community. Despite Mayor Gray's ban on parades, the veterans continued to demonstrate and could at any time touch off a violent incident.

The issue which had apparently precipitated the strike initially, collective bargaining in the contract shops, was no closer to solution. The managers resolutely refused to recognize the Metal Trades Council as bargaining agent for their employees. They were supported by Senator Robertson who knew full well that such trades councils were operating effectively in most major cities of Canada.[9] The Minister was so distraught by the alleged threat of the One Big Union that he could bring little of his experience and less impartiality to bear on the dispute.

The strike had been on for three weeks. Labour solidarity and morale had held firm. But no one had anticipated such a protracted struggle. The Citizens' Committee had managed to staff most essential services with volunteers of which there seemed an endless supply. The federal government was ranged solidly against the strike leadership. Something would have to give soon. On June 4, the Strike Committee, in an apparent attempt to force the issue, again tried to shut down the city.

Restaurants and theatres were closed once more. Milk and bread delivery-men were again called out. The following day two thousand veterans in retaliation, offered their services as special constables to defeat Bolshevism. In hindsight, the turning point of the strike had been reached.

The federal parliament, with unseemly haste, passed amendments to the Immigration Act which granted sweeping, discretionary power to the government to deport anyone who sought to overthrow constituted authority. Locally, the City Council, on June 9, dismissed the Winnipeg Police force with very few exceptions. Their places were immediately taken by special constables with no training in civilian control. The following day the first riot took place. It was luridly reported that it was precipitated by aliens. On the night of June 16-17 the *coup-de-grace* was administered by the federal government. The strike leaders, eight in number, including Russell, Johns, Queen, Ivens, and Armstrong, were arrested and charged with seditious conspiracy. Four non-Anglo-Saxons were also arrested, presumably to give credibility to the alien theme. The *Western Labour News* was suppressed. John Dafoe, the editor of the *Manitoba Free Press*, who opposed the arrests since he felt the strike was dying, predicted that the only result would be to give to labour a martyrology.

Now leaderless and disorganized, the strike collapsed. The arrested leaders were soon released on bail on the condition that they would take no further part in the strike. The climax came in one final tragic and unnecessary demonstration. The veterans who supported the strike announced that a silent parade would be held on June 21 in sympathy for the jailed leaders. The parade was broken up by two mounted charges of the North West Mounted Police. The second time they came shooting. Two people were killed and thirty injured. On June 23, Winnipeg's citizens found the downtown streets patrolled by troops with rifles and machine guns mounted on trucks.

After a gloomy and dispirited meeting the Trades and Labour Council called off the Winnipeg General Strike on June 25.

The role of the newspapers in the strike, both local and national, was almost uniformly hostile to the general strike as such. Only the *Toronto Star* seemed to have any real sympathy for, and appreciation of, the plight of workers in the immediate postwar era. It is evident, however, that editors across the country were badly frightened by the strike in its early stages. Only when it became clear that there was no violent revolution taking place in Winnipeg was there any rational discussion of the factors involved. Even then, collective bargaining was the only issue which received any judicious consideration. Otherwise, Canadian readers were given distorted and sensational editorial sermons on Bolshevism, aliens, and radical labour.

The normal political partisanship of newspapers does not seem to have been affected in the least. Traditionally Liberal journals used the strike to point out the failings and iniquities of the government. The Conservative press indulged themselves, equally, in attacks on the opposition. In Alberta, the strike quickly became just another occasion for the peculiar, internecine newspaper warfare of that province. When the strike ended and the editors unburdened themselves of their homilies, the great dailies passed on to more immediate things, as they must.

The part played by the Winnipeg press is at once more important and more interesting. The general strike was the pivotal event in the city's political history and its effects are still being felt. The newspapers played an important role in moulding attitudes and creating a continuing mythology of the strike. The three Winnipeg dailies, the *Free Press*, *The Tribune* and *The Telegram* were all shut down by the strike and it is not to be expected that they would show much understanding of the objectives of the striking workers. Their reaction ranged from frank and vigorous opposition to the hysteria of *The Telegram*.

Their assault on labour leaders in general and the Strike Committee in particular engendered a permanent sense of injury among Winnipeg's working class. The constant harping on the alien theme, especially by *The Telegram* poisoned the social atmosphere of Winnipeg, a city rich in ethnic variety.

Yet, for stridency, none of them could match *The Winnipeg Citizen*, the organ of the Citizens' Committee. At times it was simply vicious in its Red-baiting. One is even tempted to conclude that in its appeals to the returned soldiers it was consciously inciting violence in order to bring the strike to a rapid and righteous climax. The *Western Labor News*, it must be said as well, was hardly an example of independent journalism. In the weeks before the strike, its championship of the One Big Union was provocative in the extreme, as it indulged itself in epithet and recrimination on the wickedness of capitalist society.

In their way, however, both *The Winnipeg Citizen* and the *Western Labor News* were reflecting the most deeply held fears and hopes of the community. Whatever may be said of men like Russell, Johns, and Ivens, they were seeking a better world for all. Their vehicle, the One Big Union, was the still-born casualty of the general strike. Yet, it is a measure of the leaders of the strike that most of them thereafter gave many years of effective, and often distinguished, service to their community and country. They were, in the end, a pretty unlikely lot of revolutionaries. They had no real conception of how to direct a general strike let alone manage an insurrection. They stumbled erratically making day-to-day decisions, trying to cope as best they could with the multitude of problems they had created.

As for the Citizens' Committee, they had seen their city on the verge of anarchy and were determined to save it and the country from the domination of the One Big Union. The disillusionment which followed the war and their apprehension over the Russian Revolution made them fear any dramatic social departure. They sought the familiar and stable prewar world which was now gone forever. While one may not condone their overreaction to the strike, it is at least understandable.

D. C. Masters came to the conclusion that "... there was no seditious conspiracy and that the strike was what it purported to be, an effort to secure the principle of collective bargaining."[10] H. A. Robson, who was appointed by the provincial government to investigate the causes of the strike, came to a somewhat different conclusion. "It is more likely that the cause of the strike is to be found on other heads, namely, the high cost of living, inadequate wages ... profiteering."[11] Undoubtedly, these practical and very real issues played an important role in precipitating the strike. It may be suggested, however, that the overriding issue in the general strike was the One Big Union.

Both sides in the struggle had their vision of Utopia. The strikers' vision was embodied in the philosophy of the One Big Union but the tactics of the movement created an insurmountable barrier to the achievement of the workers' goal. It was not simply that the general strike was considered an alien device in a time of pronounced xenophobia but that it challenged all the current assumptions about democratic, representative government. While the general public might sympathize with the plight of the workers, they would never concede that capitalism and "British institutions" had failed and should be abandoned. The Citizens' League, and those it represented, wished to restore the world of pre-1914 with all its inequities. They were not so much conscious exploiters as captives of the free enterprise mythology which they sought to sustain.

The summer of 1919 was a brief, but vivid, nightmare for most Canadians. For Winnipeg, its legacy was bitterness, frustration, and suspicion. The general strike was over but the passions it provoked would not be allayed for many years to come.

Notes to Introduction

1 Robert K. Murray, *Red Scare* (Minneapolis: University of Minnesota Press, 1955), pp. 113-114.

2. The best estimate seems to be a 70 percent rise in living costs and 18 percent in real wages.

3. *Manitoba Free Press*, August 23, 1918; see also D. C. Masters, *The Winnipeg General Strike* (Toronto: University of Toronto Press, 1950), pp. 13-16.

4. Sidney and Beatrice Webb, *The History of Trade Unionism* (New York: A. M. Kelly, 1965), p. 656.

5. The account of the convention is based on the verbatim record published by the *Winnipeg Tribune*, April 5, 1919. See also *Ibid.*, April 15, 1919.

6. It is curious, in view of later events, that the newspapers gave little notice to the Calgary Convention. Only after the General Strike began did it receive attention from anti-labour groups.

7. *Canadian Annual Review* (1919), p. 467.

8. There is an excellent discussion of this aspect of the strike by David Bercuson, "The Winnipeg General Strike, Collective Bargaining and the One Big Union Issue," *Canadian Historical Review* (June, 1970), pp. 164-177.

9. *Ibid.*

10. Masters, *op. cit.*, p. 134.

11. *Royal Commission to Enquire into and Report upon the Causes and Effects of the General Strike which recently existed in the City of Winnipeg for a period of six weeks, including the methods of calling and carrying on such strike.* H. A. Robson, K. C., Commissioner, Winnipeg, 1919, p. 25.

Guide to Documents

SECTION I Background to the Winnipeg General Strike

SECTION II The Strike, May 16 – June 10: Its Champions and Its Critics

SECTION III The Causes and Consequences of Violence, June 10 – June 23

SECTION IV Postmortem

A Note on the Documents

Unless otherwise noted, the documents reproduced below conform, in spelling, grammatical usage and punctuation, to the originals. Since *Canadian History Through the Press* is, in a limited sense, a history of Canadian journalism, it has seemed advisable to preserve contemporary usage however questionable it might appear to be, in order to illustrate the changing quality of Canadian journalistic writing.

Section I

Background to the Winnipeg General Strike

The One Big Issue in the Winnipeg "Strike" is Plain

THE PEOPLE MUST CHOOSE

Between This ← → And This

The Alien Enemy

Who openly or secretly supported Germany and Austria during the war, who contributed money for bombs used in blowing up munitions plants on this continent, who danced for joy when the Lusitania was destroyed, who rejoiced over the long lists of Canadian casualties.

The Strike Committee, Ivens, Mrs. Armstrong, Dixon, Queen and the rest twist and squirm and lie in an effort to evade this issue. To fool the returned soldiers they say NOW: "We go on record that we will support all efforts on the part of the authorities to deport all the undesirable aliens in our midst." They ask returned soldiers NOW: "What does the alien question amount to so far as the strike is concerned? Are the strikers defending undesirable aliens? Most assuredly they are not."

The people who say this today are the same people who voted for this resolution at the Calgary convention last March:

"That the interests of all members of the international working class being identical, that this body of workers **RECOGNIZE NO ALIEN but the capitalists.**" (Endorsed by the Winnipeg Trades and Labor Council, March 18, 1919.)

They are the same people who voted endorsement to this statement, made on the floor of the Calgary convention:

"**We are asking for the release of those whom they consider as enemies, that is, actively working for the German government in this country**." (From official Calgary convention report, endorsed by almost unanimous vote by Winnipeg Trades and Labor Council March 18, 1919.)

They are the same people who say: "All strikers (including the hundreds of aliens now on strike) must be given back their jobs before we call off this strike." They are exactly the same people who did everything in their power to hinder Canada's war efforts, to prevent re-inforcements being sent overseas. They are the same people who fought conscription, tooth and nail.

They are the same people who are doing everything in their power, at the present moment, to prevent babies and invalids, including the sick returned soldiers at 'Tuxedo hospital, from obtaining milk.

There is no room in Canada for the undesirable alien who insults our flag, intimidates our citizens and demands soviet government.

The Flag

That is the symbol of law and order in this country; that guarantees to every man, woman and child in this country the right to live; that represents the authority which now enables the people of Winnipeg to get the necessities of life "without permission of the strike committee."

The Citizens' Committee of One Thousand

1 THE BIRTH OF THE ONE BIG UNION: I

The Manitoba Free Press, Winnipeg
March 14, 1919

FIRST DAY OF CONFERENCE AT CALGARY MARKED BY DRASTIC RESOLUTIONS

A resolution supporting the policy of industrial unionism and separation from the international organizations was passed amid the greatest enthusiasm at the Western Canada labor conference this afternoon and every delegate supported it earnestly on behalf of the several branches of labor represented.

The following is the detailed resolution:

"Resolved, that this convention recommend to its affiliated memberships the severance of this affiliation with their international organizations and that steps be taken to form an industrial organization of all workers, and be it further resolved that a circular letter outlining a probable plan of organization be sent out to the various organizations, and that a referendum on the question be taken at the same time and that the question be submitted to the entire Canadian membership, ballot returns to be segregated from Port Arthur as the dividing line between east and west."

A DECLARATION OF WAR.

That the passing of this resolution is an automatical [*sic*] declaration of war on the part of the labor people against the capitalistic classes of the world was the opinion of the majority of the delegates, and when Delegate J. Taylor, of Vancouver, asked if that was what the resolution amounted to he was soon set at rest by the roar of approval which surged through the hall.

Another delegate was afraid that their efforts would be put at naught by the class of labor men who would like it, but did not want it if there was any work attached to the getting of it. Now that the die was cast, it was up to everyone to roll up their sleeves and fight.

RESOLUTION STRONGLY SUPPORTED

For three hours delegate after delegate took the floor and stated why they should support the resolution, and there was hardly one dissenting voice in the whole gathering. What feeble resistance there was was beaten down by the majority after the different points had been debated on.

Man after man, in bursts of eloquence, approved of the resolution and scorned the idea of being afraid of the international trades and labor, and when the vote was taken and carried the rafters rang with the cheers and roars of the delegates.

---

2 THE BIRTH OF THE ONE BIG UNION: II

Western Labor News, Winnipeg
March 21, 1919

DELEGATES RUSSELL AND JOHNS REPORT FROM THE CALGARY CONFERENCE

WHEREAS, holding the belief in the ultimate supremacy of the Working Class in matters economic and political, and that the light of modern developments have proved that the legitimate aspirations of the labor movement are repeatedly obstructed by the existing political forms, clearly show the capitalistic nature of the parliamentary machinery, this Convention expresses its open conviction that the system of Industrial Soviet Control by selection of Representatives from Industries is more efficient and of greater political value than the present form of Government;

BE IT RESOLVED that this Conference places itself on record as being in full accord and sympathy with the aims and purposes of the Russian Bolshevik and German Spartacan Revolutions, and be it further resolved, that we demand immediate withdrawal of all Allied troops from Russia; and further, that this Conference is in favor of a General Strike on June 1st should the Allies persist in their attempt to withdraw the Soviet administration in Russia or Germany, and that a system of propaganda be carried out and that a referendum vote be taken.

Another recommendation of the Committee which was unanimously adopted and without debate read:

PROLETARIAT DICTATORSHIP

That this Convention declare its full acceptance of the principle of "proletariat Dictatorship" as being absolute and efficient for the transformation of capitalistic private property to communal wealth and that fraternal greetings be sent to the Russian Soviet Government, the Spartacans in Germany, and all definite working-class movements in Europe and the World, recognizing they have won first place in the history of the class struggle.

Yet another resolution, on which there was no discussion, and which was adopted, read:

That the interests of all Members of the Working-Class being identical, that this Body of Workers recognizes no alien but the Capitalist; also that we are opposed to any wholesale immigration of Workers from various parts of the World and who would be brought here at the request of the Ruling Class.

3 THE METAL TRADES STRIKE

The Manitoba Free Press, Winnipeg
May 2, 1919

METAL TRADE WORKERS GO OUT THIS MORNING

At 10 o'clock this morning three thousand men will be on strike in Winnipeg in the building and metal trades, the latter last night, deciding to follow the example of the building trade employees, and the ranks of the latter being swelled by the withdrawal from outside points by the building trades' council of all men hired in the city and the calling out of the mill hands.

J. R. Adair, secretary of the Metal Trades' council, in announcing the decision of these workers, said that most of the shops had turned down the schedule submitted by the contract shop employees and refused to consider the eight-hour day or abide by any decision of the Canadian War board.

When the men heard this report, he stated, they had resolved to strike work this morning.

There are approximately 1,000 men affected embraced in the following employments: Machinists, moulders, pattern makers, blacksmiths, boiler makers, bridge shopmen, electricians, helpers and laborers employed in all contract shops.

Five of the smaller shops have granted wage increases satisfactory to the union, with a proviso that these employers will be given an adjustment in keeping with the advances made the railway machinists.

James Winning, secretary of the Building Trades' council, announced last night that all mill hands, men engaged in the sash and door factories, had been called out yesterday. They number 300, and are included in the general total of 2,000 employees on strike in the building trades.

The men, Mr. Winning declared, were determined to remain out until a fair offer had been made.

A. E. Godsmark, secretary of the Builders' exchange, beyond stating there had been no new developments, would make no statement last night. He would say nothing on the question of whether an arbitration board had been sought.

The principal construction jobs temporarily held up are Tuxedo Military hospital, the new Parliament building, Fort Rouge sub-station, the roller-coaster at Winnipeg Beach, and the grand stand at River park.

The electrical workers are continuing at work at the parliament buildings.

Hon. Geo. A. Grierson, minister of public works, stated yesterday that the schedule adopted twelve months ago by the fair wages' board in relation to work on the parliament building, was still in force, no new schedule having as yet been considered.

4 THE IDEA OF A GENERAL STRIKE TAKES SHAPE

The Manitoba Free Press, Winnipeg
May 7, 1919

ALL UNIONS ASKED TO TAKE A STRIKE VOTE

The Trades' and Labor council has decided unanimously to support the striking metal workers and the workers in the building trades in their efforts to establish better wages, reduction of hours of labor, recognition of unions and collective bargaining.

"Every union affiliated with the Trades Council has been asked to take a ballot of its members with the idea of calling a general strike in support of the men of the organizations named who are at present on strike."

The above announcement was made by Ernest Robinson, secretary and business agent of Trades council at the conclusion of a meeting of that body last night, to which press representatives were not admitted.

Continuing, Mr. Robinson said: "It is anticipated that within one week, unless the employers give way, Winnipeg will be experiencing a second, and more severe, sympathetic strike.

"A special meeting of Trades council will be held next Tuesday night to put into operation, if necessary, a general strike.

"Special preparations have been made to take the strike vote in the least possible time. These votes will be taken at points convenient to the respective workers except in the cases of unions which meet in the interim. In the case of the latter, the vote will be registered at the union meeting. Arrangements were made last night for the printing of the official ballot papers."

The meeting was one of the largest in the history of the local labor parliament, the largest room in the temple being crowded to the doors with interested labor men in addition to the appointed union delegates. There was little else of public interest transacted at the meeting.

5 SYMPATHY FOR THE STRIKERS

The Telegram, Winnipeg
May 7, 1919

UNANIMOUS VOTE OF LABOR MEN FOR SYMPATHY STRIKE

Unless the demands of the striking metal trades and building trades workers are acceded to Winnipeg will be tied up by a general strike of all trades next Wednesday if the expectations of the officers of the Trades and Labor council are realized.

At a meeting of the Trades and Labor council last night a unanimous decision was reached to support the present strikers "in their efforts to establish better wages, reduction of hours of labor, recognition of unions and collective bargaining."

Every union affiliated with the Trades council has accordingly been asked to take a strike vote with the idea of calling a general sympathetic strike. The vote applies to railroad shops and running trades, to the police, firemen, street railway workers, and in fact every trades union in the city.

WILL TAKE QUICK VOTE

The council made special arrangements to get a quick vote of all unions. Where a union is holding its regular meeting this week the vote will be taken at the meeting; in the case of unions not meeting this week, arrangements have been made to have the vote taken at points convenient to the respective workers. The ballot papers were printed early this morning and are now being distributed to the workers.

E. Robinson, secretary of the Trades and Labor council, in a statement issued this morning, said: "It is anticipated that within one week, unless the employers give way, Winnipeg will be experiencing a second general sympathy strike – a more severe sympathy strike even than the last. A special meeting of the Trades and Labor council will be held next Tuesday night to put into operation, if necessary, a general strike."

Employers in the building trades contend that if they were to concede the workers' demands it would put a sudden and absolute stop to building in the city for this year. "We might say 'Yes, we'll pay you fellows all you ask,' " said a leading contractor, today, "but if we did it wouldn't benefit the workers any because they'd have no work to do. Building would be absolutely prohibitive."

Employers in the metal trades declined to make any comment on the latest development of the situation.

---

6 THE SEARCH FOR A COMPROMISE

The Telegram, Winnipeg
May 12, 1919

GENERAL STRIKE STILL POSSIBLE THROUGHOUT CITY

The great general strike determined upon in Winnipeg by overwhelming vote of trades unions, in support of the striking metal trades and building trades workers, may be averted, if renewed negotiations between the men and the employers, arranged by Mayor Gray after efforts lasting since last Friday, prove successful in bringing about a settlement.

Mayor Gray called upon the strikers last Friday and had repeated conferences with both them and their employers during the week-end, as a result of which both sides agreed to meet and negotiate once more at any time and place determined by the mayor. His worship according [sic] called a meeting in the Builders' Exchange for this afternoon at 2 o'clock, which is now in progress, with both employers and workers of both the disputing trades present. Prior to this meeting Mayor Gray visited the Trades Hall and met the workers' representatives at 1:15. A conference ensued but no details were divulged. The men's committees then proceeded with the mayor to the Builders' Exchange to meet the employers.

COMPROMISES ARE EXPECTED

It is stated upon reliable authority that the heads of the Builders' Exchange have decided to offer very substantial compromises and that the leaders of the metal trades employers have indicated a willingness to take a most conciliatory attitude with their men, so that upon the outcome of today's conference rests the entire question of whether a general strike is or is not to tie up Winnipeg.

Hopes are of the brightest for an amicable settlement being reached, but should any obstacle be put in the way and a strike be called, then Winnipeg will be without police or fire protection, waterworks or electric light employees, railroad shopmen will be involved, postmen will strike, having already voted to do so aside from their own projected strike over their own troubles. The firemen are voting today, overwhelmingly for strike, and every branch of organized labor is involved, with the exception of those unions whose internationals forbid sympathy strikes.

The situation, while giving some promise of settlement, is regarded as the most tense in the history of Winnipeg; scores of people are preparing to leave for the beaches or for their farms or summer resorts in case of the general strike being called; aldermen and employers of labor are among the number. Meantime, the mayor is leaving no stone, whatsoever, unturned and is taking practically no sleep, in his effort to avert the impending disaster.

The telephone operators are late with their vote, the ballot being taken among them on Wednesday night, though the result of the whole vote is supposed to be known to the Trades Council on Tuesday night. It is not the intention of the workers to put out trades gradually, starting Monday night, but to pull out all workers at once on Thursday, so as to exert the utmost ounce of pressure upon employers.

---

7 LABOUR REFUSES TO GIVE IN

The Telegram, Winnipeg
May 13, 1919

CONFER IN HOPE OF SETTLING

Hopes for the averting of the proposed general strike which the labor men intend to call for Thursday failing capitulation on the part of building and metal trades employers, do not appear to be brightening, and it need surprise nobody if the tie-up takes place as scheduled.

Meantime the efforts of Mayor Gray and others whom he called in to assist him, among them Premier Norris, are not being relaxed. The mayor called a special caucus meeting of the city council at noon today and laid all of the facts of the case and a history of negotiations, before the aldermen, asking for any suggestions or advice or assistance that they might be able to offer. It was agreed that his worship had done practically all in his power to avert the threatened disaster.

MEETINGS YESTERDAY

After efforts lasting over three days, the mayor got the disputing parties together yesterday afternoon, at a meeting in the Builders' Exchange offices, with Premier Norris present. Metal trades workers and employers exchanged views, as also did the building trades workers and employers. There is said to be a likelihood of the building trades dispute being adjusted before the day is out, but as much cannot be said for the metal trades dispute. Both sides to the latter are standing on what they regard as inviolable principles, and both principles are entirely opposite to one another.

Some progress was made yesterday in the five-hour conference in the Builders' Exchange, but it was with difficulty that a further conference was arranged for today. This second conference has been in progress in the Builders' Exchange offices since two o'clock this afternoon with Mayor Gray present in the meeting of the building trades disputants, and Premier Norris present at the meeting of the metal trades disputants.

E. Robinson, secretary of the Trades and Labor council, when asked for a statement, professed to be hugely surprised at the information that the mayor had been attempting to secure a settlement. In regard to the threatened walk-out, however, he said:

"While there is life there is still hope, and if the employers want to grant the men the concessions the men demand, before it is too late, well then everything will be all right, but the men themselves will absolutely not give in one inch."

---

8 GENERAL STRIKE ORDERED AT 11 O'CLOCK

The Telegram, Winnipeg
May 14, 1919

All hopes for averting the general strike called for 11 o'clock tomorrow morning, are receding. The mayor, who has worked night and day for nearly a week to avert it and who has never entirely lost hope of a settlement being reached, was far from optimistic today and when asked how the situation stood, admitted:

"Prospects for a settlement and for avoiding the threatened walkout are not bright. We have another meeting between the striking workmen and the employers this afternoon, but unless the ironmasters, the employers in the metal trades, abandon the principle they are standing on, there is no doubt that the strike will take place, for the workers will not recede from their position."

WILL MAINTAIN LAW AND ORDER

Asked as to the city's plan to meet conditions in respect to the walkout of police and firemen and employes on public utilities, Mayor Gray stated that all that he would be prepared to state at this time was: "We will keep law and order in this city. I am absolutely confident that we will keep law and order, with the co-operation of the labor men themselves, and that no citizen will imperil the interests of the city itself by committing any provocative act."

It is stated on good authority that the Trades and Labor council itself will supply men to picket and patrol the streets so far as is necessary to prevent looting, pillaging and violence.

Organized Winnipeg workers are all ordered by the Trades and Labor council, to walk out in a general strike at 11 o'clock tomorrow morning.

The Trades Council at its special meeting last night, received a report from the balloting of the past week and though no figures were given out for publication, it was announced that the vote was "overwhelmingly in favor" of a general sympathy strike.

The strike order applies to all unions affiliated with the Trades and Labor council, irrespective of whether an individual union has voted against strike and irrespective of whether certain unions have voted at all or not.

Unions which decline to obey the strike order will be dealt with at a later meeting of the Trades Council, and probably will be expelled or asked to withdraw their delegates from the Trades Council.

ALL BRANCHES OF CITY LABOR

These are the central facts of the greatest labor crisis that has ever faced the city of Winnipeg. The workers plan by massed action tomorrow morning to tie up the railroads as far as possible; the railroad shops completely; the postal service of the government, police force and the fire brigade, the city waterworks and electric light and power plant, unionized restaurants and eating-houses, the railroad works at Transcona, tailor shops, box factories, candy factories, cartage teamsters, who transport commodities from point to point in the city, telephone service, street railway service and everything throughout the whole gamut of organized labor.

At the conferences between strikers and employers arranged yesterday by Mayor Gray, a few more rays of light were let in, but not to such an extent as to warrant the hope of complete settlement. At the meeting between the building trades workers and the members of the Builders' Exchange, with Mayor Gray presiding, his worship took the situation into his own hands and actually drafted a compromise schedule of wages. The employers agreed to pay it if the men would accept. The men agreed to submit the offer to their union, which they did last night. This morning they notified the mayor that while the offer was acceptable to the union, the men would not accept it nor agree to it unless the employers in the

metal trades would give in to their employes and agree to recognize and deal with the unions through the Metal Trades council.

ISSUE UP TO METAL TRADES

This leaves the issue purely up to the metal trades. The workmen insist that the employers must deal with the unions and recognize the Metal Trades council as the official body to negotiate and bargain as to scales and working conditions. The employers are just as firm in declaring that they recognize the right to organize, that they do not discriminate against men who are members of the union, but that they will not deal with the unions as unions. '

---

9 AN APPEAL FOR LAW AND ORDER

The Manitoba Free Press, Winnipeg
May 15, 1919

MAYOR GRAY APPEALS TO CITIZENS OF WINNIPEG TO AVOID VIOLENCE

Mayor Gray, through the Free Press, appeals to the citizens of Winnipeg to act calmly during the present crisis. His worship issued the following statement last night:

To The Citizens of Winnipeg:

"During the last few days the premier and myself have done all humanly possible to bring about a settlement of the untoward conditions at present pertaining between employers and employes. We urged arbitration. When that was rejected we got the parties together several times for consultation to see if some agreement could be arrived at. This failing, we made suggestions of our own that might appeal to both sides, but all to no avail.

"The strike will possibly be on by the time that this is in print, or soon after. It is likely to be the biggest strike in the history of our city. It will vitally affect every citizen and I want to make an earnest appeal to all, the employers, the striking members of all the unions, and to that great body of the public who have no responsibility, no say, in causing this tremendous struggle, but who will suffer as a consequence.

"Citizens of Winnipeg: History has taught us that men only learn wisdom under the pressure of calamity – calmness, patience and British fair play are the salient attributes that must and will guide us safely through the trying hour in our city's life.

"I firmly believe that no one individual would willingly cause suffering to another, but the psychology of the mass, or mob, as it is more commonly called, is hard to fathom. Law and order must be the fundamental basis of our social structure, and if that one basic point is observed all others follow in its even tenor as night follows day.

"As mayor of this city, by the suffrage of the people, I wish to state most emphatically that I will not allow myself to be stampeded by any particular section of society, but will act and will only act as the occasion warrants in the interests of the people.

"I appeal earnestly for co-operation and calmness under all conditions. I firmly believe that all those various factions of employers and employes involved in this unfortunate affair will be constitutional and law-abiding.

"Should any acts be committed that savor of lawlessness I will act swiftly and surely and will use to the full the powers vested in me by the voice of the people.

"Citizens, go about your business quietly.

"Do not congregate in crowds.

"Make no provocative statements.

"And at all times realize that the constituted authorities will take all the necessary steps to ensure no radical departure from the normal, law-abiding conditions of community life."

Charles F. Gray (Mayor).

10 BOLSHEVISM IN THE ONE BIG UNION

The Gazette, Montreal
May 15, 1919

STRIKE TO-DAY AT WINNIPEG

The final conference, at which it was hoped to avert the general strike, ended late this afternoon. No settlement has been reached. Mayor Charles Gray said all his efforts had been exhausted to bring the contending parties into harmony, but without result.

James Winning, President of the Trades Council, said on coming from the meeting: "This means that the strike will become effective at 11 o'clock Thursday morning. We are at an absolute deadlock, and no further conferences have been arranged."

To be No Exceptions

Winnipeg consequently faces one of the most serious strikes in its history. The city is confronted with the prospect of having all public utilities tied up. According to Labor leaders there are to be no exceptions in this strike, and it is intimated that even the few unions which decided not to take a sympathetic strike vote must abide by the decision of the majority or run the risk of being deprived of their charter in the Labor Council. The principle of collective bargaining is at stake, they say.

Veterans to Consult

At the call of the Presidents of the G. W. V. A., the Army and Navy Veterans, and the Imperial Veterans, a mass meeting of all veterans, 16,000 in number, will be held at 8 o'clock to-morrow morning to test the attitude of returned soldiers in the event of a general strike.

The Presidents stated that they wish it distinctly understood that this is not an effort against legitimate strikes nor an effort at strikebreaking, but simply a meeting of returned men to consider how they can best co-operate with the authorities in maintaining law and order should riots develop with attendant menace to life and property. While in full accord with legitimate demands of Labor, the three Executives say that they have knowledge that there is a "Red" element in the ranks of Labor who would probably take advantage of any strike situation to foment anarchy and promote a revolution along the lines of Russian Bolshevism. It is stated that eighty unions, involving approximately 25,000 workers, will lay down their tools.

Mayor's Firm Attitude

Mayor C. F. Gray said this afternoon that in the event of a walkout he would adopt a very firm attitude in maintaining law and order. He announced his intention of addressing the firemen and policemen, pointing out that life and property must be protected at all costs.

The big utilities, water and light, it was stated at the City Hall, can be maintained, with perhaps minor difficulties. Organized Labor expects no settlement. At the Labor Temple preparations for a strike are well advanced, and a strong strike committee had been formed.

Must Adjust Every Demand

While the strike was called for the purpose of enforcing a settlement of the demands of the building trades and metal workers, once the strike is effective, Secretary Robinson announced, no settlement will be permitted until every demand of every union has been satisfactorily adjusted. Negotiations will not be permitted between employers and respective unions, but all communications are to be handled by the Strike Committee, which will have absolute authority over the strike, and will approve or disapprove any settlement offered.

Ernest Robinson, Business Agent and Secretary of the Trades and Labor Council, in a statement given out at the conclusion of last night's meeting, said that railway men had decided that in case of a general tie-up all foremen refusing to handle tools would be given the full protection of the organization. Transcona is included in the general strike.

SECTION II

The Strike, May 16 – June 10: Its Champions and its Critics

1 WINNIPEG IS FIGHTING THE ONE BIG UNION

The Gazette, Montreal
May 17, 1919

THE WINNIPEG STRIKE

The strike which is in progress in Winnipeg presents features which merit serious consideration. The trouble, which was confined previously to the metal and building trades, has become general. From fifteen to twenty-five thousand employees have left their work, and all branches of commercial and industrial activities of the city are affected. That would be sufficiently serious, but there is more. The post office employees, firemen and street railway employees, telephone, power and waterworks employees and yardmen and shopmen of the steam railways have walked out. Newspapers have been forced to suspend. This means that not only has the business of the city been paralyzed, but the public services have been abandoned, and would be completely out of commission except for the action of volunteer citizens. The Department of Labor at Ottawa has been appealed to, but the Minister of Labor has declared himself unable to act, because conciliation and arbitration have been rejected, and the workers refuse to respect the governing powers of their organizations. The employers in the metal trades, according to the statement of Mayor Gray, of Winnipeg, have expressed their willingness to arbitrate, but the employees will not consent. The situation as outlined illustrates in a very forcible manner the difficulty in the way of reaching what is called a better understanding between labor and capital. In Winnipeg, labor seeks no better understanding. It has made its demands. It has declared a strike for the purpose of having those demands acceded to, whether they be just or otherwise. Arbitration has been refused, and now an attempt is being made by means of a general sympathetic strike to club the employers into submission. Thousands of men who are on strike who have no grievances of their own and do not pretend to have any grievances. [*sic*] They are on strike for the purpose of "holding up the community" so that the workers in the trades originally affected will secure concessions which, it may be fairly inferred, they do not believe they could obtain through arbitration. To put the situation shortly, Winnipeg is fighting the One Big Union.

Organized labor in Canada as well as in the United States has recently, through many of its spokesmen, repudiated the principle of the One Big Union. They did so properly and wisely. But what is the use of rejecting the One Big Union in name and applying it in practice, as it is now being applied in Winnipeg? If the labor organizations of Winnipeg were members of the One Big Union, and were seeking to obtain better terms from the employers of Winnipeg, how else would they or could they go about it than by the means now being employed? They would do exactly what is being done now, and exactly what is being proposed by organized labor in Toronto as a means of realizing the claims of striking metal workers in that city.

It is apparent that the mayor and citizens of Winnipeg appreciate fully the real significance of this struggle, and are taking steps to protect the public interest. The question is not as to the merits of the claims put forward by the original strikers, but as to the means employed. The deliberate dislocation of commerce and paralysis of industry and transportation at the public expense is capable of description in very ugly words. Whatever merit there may have been in the claims originally put forward, the strikers have put themselves out of court by refusing arbitration and resorting to force. The municipal authorities of the western city will be justified in employing drastic measures for the protection of the public interest against this outbreak of Bolshevism, for it is nothing else. Probably a test of this sort was inevitable. It is unfortunate for Winnipeg that the test should be made there, but the situation having arisen must be met. In view of the general effect which the outcome of this struggle must have in other parts of Canada, the responsibility which rests upon Mayor Gray and his colleagues cannot be overstated.

2 THE GOVERNMENT MUST ACT

The Gazette, Montreal
May 19, 1919

Sir William Mackenzie, who returned to this city [Toronto] from New York on Saturday is strongly of the opinion that the Federal Government should immediately take action looking to the settlement of the Winnipeg Strike. "The Government should use a strong hand," he declared, "This trouble might spread over Canada, and the red flag should be taken immediately from all those exhibiting it."*

*Mackenzie was co-founder of the Canadian Northern Railway.

---

3 NOT A STRIKE—A REVOLUTION

The Winnipeg Citizen
May 19, 1919

THE STRIKE SITUATION IN WINNIPEG

This newspaper is issued because of the unquestionable necessity for placing before the great body of the citizens of Winnipeg the actual facts of the strike situation from the standpoint of the citizens themselves and in order adequately to inform them of the issue that faces Winnipeg in this, the most serious hour of her history.

It must be stated at the outset that this publication is not issued on behalf of the workers, nor on behalf of the employers, nor in opposition to either of them as such, but simply and solely in the interests of the hundred and fifty thousand or more non-participants in the issues which served as the cause of the strike – or as the excuse for it. It is issued only on behalf of the great mass of the public which is suffering from the strike's effects.

It is to the general public of Winnipeg that we speak, in stating without equivocation that this is not a strike at all, in the ordinary sense of the term – it is Revolution.

It is a serious attempt to overturn British institutions in this Western country and to supplant them with the Russian Bolshevik system of Soviet rule.

Winnipeg, as a matter of plain fact, is governed by the Central Strike Committee of the Trades and Labor Council.

At a mass meeting in Victoria Park on Friday, William Ivens, ex-preacher, a pacifist during the Great War, and now editor of the Socialist organ in this city, who is the self-styled dictator of Winnipeg, declared in a speech that Winnipeg was now under Soviet rule.

"The storm is about to break," he said. "And this time, the lightning is going to strike upward, and, not down!"

The strike had then been in progress two days. Ivens did not mean that the strike itself was the "storm" – for that had already started. The "storm" to which he referred was a determined attempt to dethrone British justice and British institutions and to permanently establish in their place the dictatorship of the Soviet – of the Bolshevik.

This does not mean that the Trades Union movement, as such, is a Bolshevik movement, nor that all of the present strikers are Bolsheviki. Hundreds, nay, thousands, of the men and women now on strike honestly believe that the strike is a demonstration of sympathy for the Metal Trades workers and the principle of collective bargaining. Incidentally, the principle of collective bargaining never was in issue; the only issue in that respect was the method of applying the principle – whether through Trades Unions or through shop committees.

That, however, is beside the point to some extent, for we do not intend to indulge in the recrimination-breeding pastime of "looking backward." Winnipeg has to look forward and face the real issue that is at stake.

Bolshevism and the rule of the Soviet, or British institutions and democratic constitutional government? – That is the question for every true citizen of Winnipeg to ask, and to answer, for this is the parting of the ways.

Let us, then, examine the situation as it exists today.

Why is it that one finds thousands of men

and women among the strikers who state quite frankly that they had no wish to strike – that they did not want to strike; and yet, paradoxically, they are on strike?

It is because the "Red" element in Winnipeg has assumed the ascendancy in the Labour movement, dominating and influencing – or stampeding – the decent element of that movement, which desires the preservation of British institutions, yet is now striking unconsciously against them.

To those who think that the mere dickering of trades unions for schedules is in issue and that the strike is a strike for higher wages, for shorter hours, for better working conditions, for the "closed shop" or even for the principle of collective bargaining, we say that it is no longer that.

It ceased to be anything of the sort from the very moment that the first Trades Union struck work in sympathy with the previous strikers on Thursday, May 15, at 11 a.m. From that hour the dictum of the Central Strike Committee became effective, viz., that no one union would return to work until all of the current demands and disputes of every union were conceded by all employers.

Let us take that at its face value. Who, for one moment, imagines that this condition would end if the strike were settled at this moment by all demands of all unions being granted in full? Does anybody think that such a course would prevent a repetition of this dictatorship?

Or would it not strengthen the "Reds" and enable them to do the same thing over again whenever they felt like it – and in this connection do not forget for one instant that another general strike of all organized labor is definitely set for July 1 – a strike for a six-hour working day.

Let us repeat – this is not a strike; it is just plain ugly revolution. Two-thirds of the Unions now on strike have struck in defiance of their Internationals, knowing that they sacrifice strike-pay and that they lose all the benefits they have been paying for for thirty or forty years. They have burned their bridges behind them; the railroad unions have been expelled from their Internationals. What do they hope to gain by this? They knew, that is the Reds among

them knew, quite definitely, what they hoped to gain – the destruction of the present industrial system and the present system of government, so let nobody for one moment imagine that any degree of famine or starvation will drive them back to work. Instead, it will drive them to excesses, if the lessons of history are any guidance.

In a strike bulletin issued on Sunday, the strikers were warned to lay in stocks of foodstuffs and be prepared to stand pat until the ends of the "Reds" had been attained. Citizens should take the same advice, as to foodstuffs, to defeat this revolution.

It is seriously to be feared that the strike cannot much longer be controlled and lawlessness averted. At the outset of the strike a signed statement was issued by the heads of the Central Strike Committee, smugly urging law and order. On the second day of the strike Ivens proclaimed that Winnipeg was controlled by a Soviet.

Winnipeg citizens can learn a lesson as to what law and order is likely to be kept, and as to what strike committee rule means, by taking the first harsh act of the Committee of Winnipeg as an example. That first act was to cut off the supply of bread and the supply of milk, not only from the citizens at large, but from their own people as well! This is the sort of harsh terrorism and blind brutality that Soviet rule has meant in Russia.

And then what? The committee found itself starving the strikers and "ordered" or "permitted" its bakers, milk workers and drivers to return to work, at a certain hour. At that hour there was not a pint of milk in the creameries and not a baker in the bakeries. Thousands of gallons of milk soured on the station platforms; thousands of loaves of bread were allowed to spoil.

The moral is that a Soviet cannot even control its own adherents and is utterly unfitted to rule or govern anything. It rests only with the citizens of Winnipeg to defeat the Soviet idea.

How is this to be accomplished? The Reds dominate the 25,000 strikers and through them the 150,000 or more members of the general public. How is it that 25,000 men can dominate and dictate to 150,000 people? Solely because those 25,000 are organized and the 150,000 are not.

The only way to defeat Bolshevism is for the people, the injured, the sufferers, those who are put to hardship through this strike, those who stand in the position of the proverbially "innocent bystander" who always gets shot in a riot, to organize. They must consolidate and stand solidly behind those public-spirited bands of citizens who are protecting the city from fire, who are helping the constituted authorities in every possible manner – and they must be prepared to answer the call at any time when necessary to defend and uphold the free institutions under which we live.

---

4 WINNIPEG'S STRIKERS ARE NOT REVOLUTIONARIES

The Sun, Vancouver
May 19, 1919

WINNIPEG AND SEATTLE

Although there is a superficial resemblance between the labor troubles at Winnipeg and those which occurred recently at Seattle, the difference is nevertheless fundamental.*

In Seattle a distinct attempt was made to overturn the existing industrial system and to substitute therefore a method of Soviet control. In its essence the movement was revolutionary.

Nothing of that sort is going on at Winnipeg. There the question in dispute is simply whether the employer has or has not the right to prevent his shop from being unionized.

An employer who insists on saying who shall represent the men, is very much in the position of a litigant undertaking to select his opponent's lawyer. The claim is entirely untenable. It is a relic of old and rapidly disappearing conditions and there can be no prospect of industrial peace until it is abandoned.

At the same time, it looks as if the strike leaders in Winnipeg had allowed the intoxi-

cation of power to go to their heads. Many crafts have been called out, although they were working under agreements which they considered quite satisfactory. The employer may well wonder what is the use of making an agreement at all if it is to be wantonly broken at the employee's whim.

*Seattle was the scene of a similar general strike in the spring of 1919. [ed.]

---

5 ORGANIZED BOLSHEVISM IN WINNIPEG

The Telegraph, Quebec
May 19, 1919

THE WINNIPEG STRIKE

The general strike in Winnipeg exposes a most critical and cankerous condition in the industrial life of Canada. It is the first tangible expression of organized Bolshevism which this nation has yet been called upon to meet. For it must be distinctly understood that this is not an ordinary trade-union movement. It is not the legitimate strike of a group of laborers in order to remedy the conditions of their work. From the nature of the present strike, and from the information which can be gathered, it is apparent that this is the first triumph of the "One Big Union" movement which is being organized by Bolshevist agitators, and which the local Typographical Union recently exposed and rejected.

The general strike which has now been called in Winnipeg is inflicting untold suffering upon the whole community, rich and poor alike, but especially the poor. The suspension of the delivery of milk and bread and the collection of garbage, for instance, are terrible menaces to the health of the people, particularly infants and children. In paralyzing the whole industrial life of Winnipeg, no one stands to suffer more than the working classes themselves. We are sure that thousands of the men now on sympathetic strike, with the idea that they are helping their fellow workers, would rise up in indignation if they realized that they are being duped by cunning Bolshevist propagandists who aim at making Canada another Russia. The Winnipeg journal of the "One Big Union" declared only two or three weeks ago for a "proletarian dictatorship." Is this the sort of thing the workmen of Canada want? We think not. For the first practical step which this temporary dictatorship has taken in Winnipeg is to deprive the people of the necessities of life, and to choke public opinion by gagging the freedom of the press.

---

6 NO SOVIET AT WINNIPEG

The World, Vancouver
May 20, 1919

It is not correct to say that Soviet control has replaced civil government in Winnipeg. What has happened is merely that through the withdrawal of the trade unionists from their usual occupations the leaders of labor associations are temporarily in a position to dominate the city's commercial and industrial activities.

Soviet control is a very different thing. As practised in Russia, Soviet control means the power of life and death over a whole community. There is no power above the Soviet except a central authority in which all Soviets are represented. There are no laws except those which the Soviets pass and can enforce.

In Winnipeg the law, British law, is still in force and enforceable. If there is any attempt to break that law the consequences will be visible within the hour. There is still government control of the city. The provincial government and the Dominion government remain supreme. No one in Winnipeg is deprived of his vote or his civil status because he does not happen to belong to a trade union. Which is what happens in Russia.

Loose talk of Bolshevism in connection with labor disputes is ill-advised. Especially when those who talk loosely do not know what Bolshevism really is.

7 SCOTCH THE SNAKE

The Intelligencer, Belleville
May 20, 1919

The news from Winnipeg that a Soviet Government had been established there came as a shock to all loyal Canadians. "Soviet" in this instance may be a mere name, but it indicates an intention to seize the city if possible and govern it under the principles of Lenine and Trotzky [sic], the Judases who betrayed Russia for German gold, and are sinking Russia in a sea of blood and infamy.

Without a doubt the principle of Bolshevism and I.W.W.* has been applied to the Winnipeg situation as the result of a deep-laid plot, the aftermath of coups which failed in the United States, but with the Hidden Hand of the alien cleverly concealed. News despatches say that Germans and Austrians and other aliens in Winnipeg are keeping in the background now that they have such willing accomplices in those who pass for Canadians.

Winnipeg, that beautiful city, built up by the brain and brawn of real Canadians, is now in danger of being destroyed by dreamers with distorted vision – already immeasurable damage has been done to the city and the nation by the senseless action of a clique which succeeded in turning a live city into a corpse overnight, defying all law and authority and disregarding instructions of individual labor unions. The only sanity, seemingly, which remained in organized labor in Winnipeg, was among the prnters [sic], who refused to join the movement, although the instigators managed to make it impossible for the newspapers to issue, and frankly said that the press must be muzzled to permit the accomplishment of their designs.

That surely was enough to indicate the drift of the plot which has culminated in a proclamation of Lenine-Trotzky principles.

Clerical Visionary.

Strange to say a clerical visionary is head of the Winnipeg Bolsheviki – a retired minister whose pacifist utterances during the war, it is said, lost him his church and lured him into radical journalism.**

Declare Martial Law.

Canada wants no Bolshevism and will welcome the most drastic measures to cope with the Winnipeg situation where the civic authorities have evidently been lax enough to allow the movement to spread until the agitators thought the city was theirs. If the city can not handle the situation – and from this distance it looks to have fallen down already – the military authorities should step in at once and declare martial law, dealing with a strong hand and quickly with these un-Canadians who have dared to raise the Red Flag of Bolshevism in Canada's finest city.

Liberty Abused.

Tolerance has been abused, free speech and Canadian liberty of action have been used by cunning criminal alien agitators to sow the seeds of dissension in an effort to destroy Canada, and the time has come for all loyal Canadians, proud of our splendid country and free institutions to rally around the foundation stone of law and order and fight if need be to stamp out this evil which threatens the life, liberty and happiness of all.

Just one glance at tortured, bleeding Russia, starving and terror-stricken, where even the honor and respect of womankind has been scrapped along with all other high ideals to make a holiday for the tools of the Huns who have wrecked the country, is enough.

Prompt and Drastic Measures.

The Dominion Government can not afford to allow the civic authorities of Winnipeg to dally with the situation longer and if effective measures have not been taken ere now it is up to the Government to take charge of the situation, eliminate the poison, remove the muzzle from the press, and start all essential industries at once – with soldiers if necessary. Canadians will forgive no weak measures now, for success of Bolshevism in Winnipeg means similar periods of terrorism for every city in Canada.

*International Workers of the World.
**Apparently a reference to Rev. William Ivens.

8 CLEAN OUT THE BOLSHEVISTS

The Times, Toronto
May 20, 1919

Winnipeg is a warning to the rest of Canada. The object of the One Big Union is plain. It is the aim of the Reds who dominate that organization to use mass-power, in defiance of agreements, for the overturning of organized society. It is mere naked Bolshevism, the establishment of Soviet rule; peaceably if possible, but by force if necessary. Such a plan for strangling the life of the country and sacrificing the comfort of women and children for a visionary well-being is more than disorder. It is rebellion. We do not believe that Organized Labor in Eastern Canada will show itself the fatuous plaything of the extreme Socialists and of the German agents who are financing them.

The Times agrees with Major-General McRae that there should be a "clean up" of the revolutionary agitators and foreign undesirables who infest the country. The men who are trying to wreck society should be given notice to leave the Dominion by a certain date and either jailed or deported if they do not act accordingly. The institutions of this country, the welfare and happiness of its women and children must not be exposed to the dangers of Bolshevism. Canada must not become a second Russia. Plunder, murder and rape must not become ruling principles under the British flag. Organized Labor must not be overturned and submerged by the enemies of civilization. The Government must act with a strong hand to save the day.

9 THE LABOR CHURCH'S HOLY TRINITY

Western Labor News, Winnipeg
May 20, 1919

SURGING THRONG PACKS CHURCH IN INDUSTRIAL BUREAU

"I never saw a meeting like this in my life before. It's wonderful." Thus spake one railroader who formed part of the surging mass in the Labor church in the Industrial bureau on Sunday night. Scarce a seat in the great auditorium was vacant, and at the back, many stood.

Winnipeg has never had a church service like it in all her history. It was throbbing with interest and enthusiasm. The people felt that here was one church that really did voice their sentiments at this hour and they thronged the place. Here and there could be seen the faces of the employers. There were present also those who were sent to bring a report to the powers that be. Surely the report they must make will tell greatly for the settlement of the strike.

One enthusiastic auditor said: "I attended my church this morning, and at the close there came a call for volunteers for the 90th militia to keep order. I could scarce keep silence. We need no militia to keep us quiet. But that finishes me for churches. My letter will be returned tomorrow." Another rushed up and said to the pastor of the labor church: "I had cut out the churches. I was disgusted. But this for mine. Put me down as a member. This is what I have been looking for for years."

With such a spirit as this in the air Mr. T. F. Watts announced the opening hymn. It expressed the deepest longings of the workers, and the volume of harmony that rose from those thousands of throats in confidence, idealism, were instinctive.

President Jas. Winning Speaks

After a prayer, in which Rev. Ivens voiced the desire that the workers might succeed according to the justice of their cause, and fail so far as their demands were unjust, Mr. James Winning, President of the Trades and Labor Council gave an inspiring address.

This, said he, is a congregation to be envious of. I guarantee that many a preacher in this city would look upon it with desiring eyes. The reason you are here is because you want the TRUTH. If the preachers would come to the Labor Temple they would find the truth there.

The strike was caused by the inadequacy of the pay envelope to last to the end of the week. The wife found that it was exhausted by Wednesday night and she demanded that John ask the boss for more money. When he did this he was "fired." Hence he had to form a union to compel a rise of wages. Prices rose at the will of the boss. But he never volunteered a raise of wages. This always had to be compelled. This was possible only by organization. Bacon and Pork Trusts, Milling Profiteers, etc. were not content with normal profits. They heaped up profits and these profits brought the desire for still more profits.

Who Caused the Strike

Facing these facts, it was not hard to understand who caused the strike. The profiteer refused to recognize the men's organizations, and were unwilling to give him [sic] a living wage, though they admitted the justice of his [sic] demands. There was but one solution. The profiteer and the government that allowed the profiteering. (Thunderous applause). [sic]

The worker must get a more equitable share of the wealth of the world. And this strike had already demonstrated the ability of the worker to get his if he would consolidate his forces. Withdraw your labor power from the machine, said he, and at once profits cease.

STARVATION HEADED OFF

The constructive intelligence at the Labor Temple had headed off starvation during the past few days. There were those who would starve the workers into submission, but they must and would prevent this.

No official at the Labor Temple has anything to hide. We can say everything from the public platform.

He then outlined the struggle from the

standpoint of the building trades and the metal trades, and traced the progress of the strike to date.

THE PRESS CHOKED

The greatest victory the strikers had achieved was the choking of the daily press. (Applause). [sic] No greater victory had ever been achieved even in Glasgow – where I come from. (Laughter). [sic] There was no vindictiveness in this move. But the press had started its campaign of misrepresentation and it had to be choked. The day had gone when the bosses could get one branch of Labor to malign another part. The day had come when one branch of Labor was ready to take up the defence of every other part of Labor.

IRON POTENTATES – HOLY TRINITY

HE was speaking in a church and so must speak in terms of holiness, so he would talk of the HOLY TRINITY, or the IRON POTENTATES – Barrett, Deacon, and Warren. These men had for years defied labor and said they would never recognize organized labor. They demanded that they be autocrats in their own plants and that all others therein be serfs.

Barrett had said recently that he was converted (laughter). He was now willing to meet a committee of three men elected from the workers in his shop. But this was not recognizing the right of labor to organize. He must come much further yet. Either he must be beaten to the point where he recognizes unreservedly the right of labor to form any effective organization it desires, or labor must be wiped off the map. There could be no compromise, and there would be none.

PERFECT ORDER MAINTAINED

Some people were talking of possible riots. This was ludicrous. There was not anywhere on earth a more docile people than the workers of this city. There will be no mob violence. Keep your head cool just because there are those who would like you to lose your temper.

SECRETARY ROBINSON SPEAKS

These are tremendous times, said Sec. E. Robinson. Much has happened since Thursday last. The Trades Council had had to call upon the most terrible and the most damnable weapon it had – The General Strike. Not because they so desired, but to demonstrate to the employers that Labor as a whole had been driven to the point of extremity. Endurance has been exhausted. The strike had been forced upon Labor, and the workers had responded because today they are enlightened and understand their position in society. This strike is an indication to the employers that labor will stand no more.

THE MAN OF GALILEE

Mr. Ivens had read from the OLD BOOK. That book told of miracles performed by the MAN of Galilee. The day of miracles was not past. Miracles were taking place these days at James Street. Brotherhood was there triumphant. It was each for all and all for each. A few had asked the help of their fellows, and that call had been heard, and the response was the tramp of thousands of feet to their rescue. It was questionable whether so complete a response had ever been seen in any country at any time to the call of Labor.

---

10 FOREIGNERS: THE ROOT OF THE TROUBLE

The Telegraph, Quebec
May 21, 1919

The Winnipeg situation emphasizes the menace to a nation, such as Canada, which inheres in the free admission of foreign immigration without a careful system of government scrutiny and examination. Canada most emphatically wants immigrants. There is no doubt of that. But at the same time she does not want that element of foreign agitators whose nihilistic hysteria may be the natural product of the unfortunate lands from which they come, but who are certainly entirely out of their proper element in the free atmosphere of British institutions which they can neither understand nor appreciate.

One of the American speakers at the Good Roads Congress last evening aroused much applause by his declaration that the foreign element must be shipped out of the United States. He referred, of course, not to all foreign immigrants, but to that undesirable aggregation of propagandists who, often with German inspiration, cause so much of the trouble existing in the United States. The records show that the overwhelming majority of the law-breakers of the United States are foreigners. Uncle Sam has his own little problem to handle.

What of Canada? Are we sowing the seeds of a new trouble? So far as can be seen, the Government is doing nothing to prevent it. Where are its immigration officials, and secret service officers, that it is allowing the country to be infested with these Bolshevik foreigners? Why, above all, has it allowed these Germanophile agitators the wonderful leverage afforded by the high cost of living, against which nothing has been done? If the Government had been less solicitous of the welfare of the profiteers, and more careful in eliminating obnoxious foreign pamphleteers, the country would be in a less precarious position to-day; and such a dangerous condition as that now existing in Winnipeg would probably never have arisen. The Government owes the people an explanation.

11 "OUR CAUSE IS JUST"

Western Labour News, Winnipeg
May 21, 1919

Never have the workers of Winnipeg had so much confidence in their cause as today. Never has there been such unanimity as to absolute necessity of settling once [and] for all the two points at issue, namely:
1. THE RIGHT TO COLLECTIVE BARGAINING, and
2. THE RIGHT TO A LIVING WAGE.

Let us take the case of the men who first came on strike to try and enforce their demands.

We reproduce from the Western Labor News of May 2nd, the statement as it affects the Building Trades Strike as it affected, at that time, some 1,400 workers:

Wages only 18 per cent Higher than in 1914 – Cost of living up 80 per cent. – Bosses say Demands of men reasonable and necessary to maintain standard of citizenship – But others must take responsibility for increase men demand. – Blanket Increase of 20 cents an hour.

All workers including the Building Trades Council went on strike on Thursday morning, May 1st, after holding in the Convention Hall of the Industrial Bureau, the greatest meeting in the history of the Building Trades Council. The vote was 1,199 for strike to 74 against.

A. E. Godsmark secretary of the Building Trades Association states that "the firms have reached the limit of their ability to pay with the proposal they had submitted to the men." The following figures do not bear out his contention. The fact is, that, while building expenses have increased 35 to 40 per cent, during the war, the wages of the men have increased on the average of all trades involved only 18 per cent. An increase of only 18 per cent in wages while the cost of living has increased 80 per cent, proves both the justice of the present demands of the men and their lack of responsibility for the added cost of building construction.

The average increase offered by the master builders is 15 1/3 per cent, while the men are determined on a flat increase of 20 cents per hour, or approximately 32 per cent on present prices. This still leaves them considerably worse off than before the war. This is the reason the bosses themselves admit that the claims of the men are reasonable and justified. But, they say, other persons than the builders must bear the responsibility of increasing the cost of construction. The defence of the worker is that he is worthy of his hire and he must have a living wage.

12 THE UNION JACK vs. THE RED FLAG

The Star, Montreal
May 21, 1919

THE REAL ISSUE

The real fight at Winnipeg is not between labor and capital now, but between loyal labor and Bolshevism.

There is no doubt that the majority of the men on strike believe they are fighting for the rights of labor against oppression. There is no doubt that the great majority of those in the ranks of Canadian Labor who sympathize with their comrades out West are of the same mind. But the evidence is indisputable that the Winnipeg situation is drifting into the control of hands that are red with revolution – into the hands of fanatical men who are not working for a fairer deal for labor or for a closer co-operation for the common good of Labor and Capital, but for a complete overthrow of existing institutions, industrial, social and political; for the hauling down of the Union Jack and the hoisting of the red flag of Bolshevistic dictatorship.

Under this overshadowing menace the initial issues of the Winnipeg labor dispute have been clouded and obscured. This is particularly unfortunate from the labor standpoint as, viewed from this distance, the Metal Trade strikers had a case which enlisted a good deal of public sympathy, chiefly because of the statement that the employers had refused to negotiate with them. The official demands on which the settlement of the strike still hinges – recognition of the union and reinstatement of the strikers – are certainly not big enough to warrant the great public hardships this strike is involving. But the issue precipitated by these claims has grown so far beyond them that citizens are forced to take sides in the trouble on the broader issue without regard to the justice or injustice of the original dispute.

This is a British country based and developed on the broad principles of British democracy. The vast majority of its people are loyal to the British flag and British institutions. Admitting the existence of industrial and social inequalities and evils, they recognize that in British democratic principles, properly applied, a proper remedy may be found. Their goal is the co-operation of all classes in the community for the common good. They will resent and oppose proletariat dictatorship as strongly as Prussian dictatorship. They have not fought this war for freedom to submit at the end of it to a tyranny as bitter as that which they have overthrown.

Representatives of the Federal Government are in Winnipeg today. They should have been there a week ago. If the strikers can still be brought under the control of their sane majority of moderate folk and will confine the issue of the original quarrel, it is the duty of this Government to bring the original parties together, even if they have to us [*sic*] force to do so. But if the Bolshevik element controls there can be no compromise. Its chosen weapon is the sword, and by the sword it must perish, lest the whole country be maddened with this ages-old and oft-exploded heresy and go roaring down the heights which heretofore we have climbed, backward down to the sea of national ruin.

---

13 THE ONE BIG ISSUE

The Winnipeg Citizen
May 22, 1919

[This paper issued WITHOUT permission of the Strike Committee]

THE ONE BIG ISSUE –
is *NOT*, shall Trades form Unions – it is *NOT* collective bargaining

BUT – IS EVERY INDIVIDUAL DISPUTE BETWEEN EMPLOYER AND EMPLOYEE TO CONTINUE TO DISRUPT THE LIFE OF THE WHOLE COMMUNITY?

That, fellow-citizens, is the ONE BIG ISSUE, and it must and will be solved now by the community as a whole, once and for all.

The whole city is throbbing with indignation at being "PERMITTED TO LIVE" by a coterie of five men at the Labor Temple.

So strong is the feeling that delegation after delegation has appeared before the "Citizens Committee of One Thousand" urging immediate action.

The people of this city are not going to be forced into the position of taking sides with employer and employee.

They are not against organized labor as such. But they strenuously object to having their bread shut off, their milk shut off, their water supply threatened, their mail stopped, at the will of five individuals who do not represent constituted authority.

NO GROUP OF INDIVIDUALS HOWEVER WISE IN NEW THEORIES ARE GOOD ENOUGH TO DICTATE TO THEIR FELLOW BEINGS.

SETTLE THE TROUBLE NOW OR GO THROUGH WORSE ON JULY FIRST.

THE DECENT MEN IN LABOR CIRCLES WERE MISLED INTO THIS STRIKE DON'T BLAME THEM.

HAS IT OCCURED TO YOU THAT WINNING, VEITCH, ROBINSON AND COMPANY ARE DRAWING THEIR PAY WHILE YOU WALK STREETS.

IS CONSTITUTED AUTHORITY OR THE BOLSHEVIKI TO RULE WINNIPEG?

LET US SETTLE "THE ONE BIG ISSUE" ONCE AND FOR ALL

WINNIPEG REFUSES TO LIVE "BY AUTHORITY OF STRIKE COMMITTEE"

SHALL BABIES STARVE AND INVILADS [sic] SUFFER "BY PERMISSION OF THE STRIKE COMMITTEE"?

14 THE SAME OLD GAME

Le Soleil, Quebec
May 22, 1919 [translation]

Last night's telegrams, as those of this morning, concerning the Winnipeg strike, have just confirmed in the most decisive way the suspicion we voiced yesterday: there has not up to now been the slightest shred of evidence to support the accusations of Bolshevism thrown out by certain newspaper reporters: the situation in Winnipeg is the exact opposite of the Soviet regime since the most satisfactory calm continues to reign, not a single arrest has been made in recent days and that in reality complete tranquillity now exists in Winnipeg.

Once again we must note the baneful role, played consciously or not by a certain press, certain news agencies under the pretext of "informing public opinion."

These publicity organs in fact serve only to deceive public opinion rather than enlighten it; they seem to have become tools in the hands of certain interests well able to use them, maintaining and exploiting prejudices against all those hostile to them or their designs.

This is something that we in the province of Quebec know a little about: it is evidently the same game going on today with regard to the Winnipeg strikers.

Let no one mistake: for the time being we are reserving our opinion on the merits of the Winnipeg strike until we can fully analyse the exact facts of the case.

But one thing is certain as of this moment and that is that this enormous strike, involving more than 35,000 men and women, has shown a perfectly disciplined organization careful to keep the peace.

To speak plain then it all boils down to a conflict of interest between employers and employees, between a whole working class and their bosses: nothing more.

It seems that what has to be done is to get recognition of the union principle and regulate certain working conditions.

The movement has been powerfully organized; and we maintain that in the face of that strength the employers, or at least some of them, have resorted to an all too common manoeuvre: through the press they have sought to forestall outside public opinion, to prejudice it against the strikers by depicting them in spurious Bolshevik colours.

It must be admitted that this slander campaign has been obligingly sanctioned by certain public authorities, delighted to be able, by means of these false images, to distract public attention from those really responsible for a situation provoked in large part by the negligence and incompetence of these same officials.

The Toronto *Mail and Empire* has been eager to thunder against "anarchists, hostile foreigners and other firebrands" whom it denounces as the real instigators of all the trouble and of a supposed lawlessness which does not exist!

But if, in fact, amongst the strikers there are inevitably to be found a few workers who are foreign, i.e. not Anglo-Saxon, the known facts establish in the most definite manner that this strike is not being led by supposed anarchists from abroad but, on the contrary, by a group of Anglo-Saxons.

The Winnipeg police and postmen who have joined the strike are almost all Anglo-Saxons, Canadians, and the sympathetic or at least neutral attitude of the Winnipeg veterans demonstrate how untrue are the stories in the *Mail and Empire*.

Even our own local right wing paper has tried to get into the act so as to take advantage of these false reports.

Yesterday with comical speed it seized upon those rumours of Bolshevism to smear Mr Mackenzie King whose very shadow terrifies it. The paper tried to discredit him because some time ago he stated that "no Bolshevik threat existed in Canada."

Unfortunately, Mr Mackenzie King was proved correct: the peaceful behaviour of the Winnipeg strikers, now known and established, has just brought our fellow newspaper to its senses.

From all this we have to realize that those who bear the terrible responsibility for the situation now existing in Canada, namely our rulers and their supporters, would like, impenitent and incompetent though they are, to continue to play the same old role in spite of so much evidence against them; they hope in carrying on to the furthest limits their present slander campaign with the aid of certain organs of the press to distract public attention once again from the real state of things and to avoid their own responsibility.

But "the jug that goes too often to the well will break" and the cracked Unionist jug will soon fall into pieces no matter what is done to conceal the truth.

From one coast to the other the Canadian people are weary of a government which has neither known how nor wished to do any-thing to remedy the ills suffered by the masses.

15 THE WORKERS HAVE DECLARED WAR

The Post, Sydney, N.S.
May 22, 1919

WINNIPEG'S ONE BIG STRIKE.

This country has never experienced any situation comparable to that which has been created by the great Winnipeg strike. Originating in a dispute between the metal-workers and building-trades and their employers, spreading later to the street car employees, who demand that their pay be doubled, the strike finally embraced virtually all the working population of Winnipeg, including even the city employees, whose differences with the civic authorities had quite recently been amicably and satisfactorily adjusted. In all there are fully 30,000 men in the ranks of the strikers, who now have the entire population of the city at their mercy. Building operations involving $20,000,000 worth of construction work have been tied up. The newspapers have ceased publication. The telegraph and telephone services have been virtually discontinued. The distribution of ice, milk, bread, and other food supplies, has in some sections been discontinued altogether and throughout the entire city been so reduced as to create distressing and alarming conditions.

The question on all sides is, What does it all mean? Among the striking groups are trades which have no apparent grievance, and others which had been out on strike quite recently, had had their demands complied with, and returned to work. But last week's big strike, like a great epidemic sweeping over the city, brought them all within its radius, and reconverted them into strikers, with no apparent object but to add to the impressiveness of a vast demonstration of voluntary unemployment.

Advices from Winnipeg say that the purpose of this demonstration is to illustrate the efficacy of the "one big union" scheme, which has considerable support in the West. There is an echo of the Soviet plan of government in the usurpation of civic authority by the strikers' central committee. The assumption of control of the city's bread supply by the strikers, and their denial of the right of any to distribute it but men wearing union labels, are manifestations of Bolshevism of the Moscow and Petrograd brand. Their declaration that no newspapers shall be allowed to issue during the strike also shows close imitation of Bolshevist methods. Nothing could be more disastrous to the country's future than the success of a strike so conceived, so unjustified, and so lawlessly conducted. It is nothing less than a declaration of war by the manual workers against the civic government and the rest of the population of Winnipeg. Apparently there have as yet been no overt acts of violence on such a scale as to warrant the Government in calling on the Militia to enforce order and protect persons and property. But the situation is one which calls for immediate measures of the strongest character by the Federal authorities. It is one in which civic government has been rendered impossible, and the entire population of one of the greatest of Canada's cities placed at the mercy of a band of strikers, whose leading spirits are aliens, and in whose ranks are to be found the most dangerous elements in the country. If there is no existing statute to meet such an unprecedented situation, the Government will have to take authority to deal with it by order-in-council, under the war-measures act, which is still in force. And the general opinion in the country will be that this should have been done, without being proceded by such dickering as the Federal authoritie [sic] are now carrying on at Winnipeg.

16 UNIONISM DESTROYS INDIVIDUALISM

The Gazette, Montreal
May 22, 1919

THE WINNIPEG STRIKE.

The dimensions of the labor strike in Winnipeg have been a rude shock to the people of Canada. It was unthinkable that in this democratic country the social life of any large community could be interrupted, its business blocked, its industries prostrated, municipal services dislocated and civic government paralyzed, at the mandate of Trades Union leaders; yet that is what has happened. Labor has boasted of its power, and labor has given an example of its power of which the most dangerous feature is that it may become infectious. The strike of the metal workers was not in itself a matter of great moment, and sooner or later would have been adjusted. The disturbing thing is the sympathetic strike, the cessation from work of all the members of all the unions not because of grievances of their own but to coerce the metal trade employers into granting the demands of their employees, and inferentially to give warning that the Labor Unions are conducted on the principle of all for one and one for all. It is futile to exclaim that the whole proceeding is wrong in ethics and economics, and that none suffer in greater relative degree than the laborers who voluntarily deprive themselves of work and pay. Labor neither philosophizes nor inclines to logic. It presents demands on a bludgeon, and if the demands are not acceded to the workshop is closed and so picketed that none can enter, because a basic rule of unionism is the destruction of individualism, suppression of the will of the individual.

In the last five years what is colloquially termed labor has made an immense stride forward. The cataclysm of war gave an impetus, high wages added an influence, and revolutionary propaganda coming from Russian and German sources sowed seeds of unrest and perverted conceptions, the consequences of which are seen in Winnipeg. Labor has rights, labor has privileges, and the rights and privileges of labor were never so much regarded as now. President Wilson spoke by the book when he declared that the question which stands before all others in every country is the question of labor, the creation of a community of interest between capital and labor, shortening hours of work, paying wages that will enable the worker to live in tolerable comfort, better fed, better housed, better clothed, better schooled than he has been. Governments everywhere are seeking to attain this end. The eight-hour day is in force quite generally in Great Britain, and on this continent. Public money is being devoted to prevent unemployment, and schemes for old age pensions, insurance against sickness, the prevention of child labor, better sanitary surroundings in factories are engaging the earnest study of legislators. It is under these circumstances when labor may look hopefully for the dawn of a better day that the attempt is made to set up in Winnipeg Soviet government after the Russian pattern.

We do not believe for a moment that the people of Canada will tolerate the autocratic rule of the unions, whose combined membership is not a very large proportion of the population. Labor leaders, however, Rev. Mr. Ivens for instance, retort "What are you going to do about it?" And if the strikers refrain from overt act [sic] of criminality, the answer is not obvious. Unionism of labor is lawful, and there is no compulsion upon unwilling men to work. But there are silent forces operating always to restore order and normality; the moral influence of the people at large, the conscience of many strikers, and the pangs of hunger. If capital cannot coerce labor, neither can labor coerce capital. There is a limit set to the wage scale, namely, the ability to market the product of labor at profitable price. Some revolutionists talk of limiting hours of work to six, or even four hours, of fixing wages at a high minimum, and of restricting production to actual necessities of the people, as if a Chinese wall could be built about Canada and a new Heaven and a new earth made therein. Madmen who preach these doctrines will not long hold their congregation, and it will be a proper act for the Govern-

ment to invite them to return to the countries whence they came. But the Canadian workingman has at bottom sufficient saving grace of sense not to embrace the pernicious teaching of Bolshevism, and to realize that the high cost of living which has given him unrest and dissatisfaction is not to be reduced by increasing the cost of production.

It is sometimes asked: "Why does not the Government intervene and settle the Winnipeg trouble?" Those who put the question ignore the fact that the Government is but another name for the people, that it derives all its functions and powers from the people. Law and order must be maintained if Canada is not to relapse into a state of anarchy; and with the first outbreak of violence in Winnipeg – which may Heaven avert – the duty of prompt action will be laid upon the Government. Swift should be the action to punish and repress, confident in the sanity and support of the overwhelming mass of the Canadian people.

It may be that press despatches give too lurid a color to the situation, but even allowing for exaggeration, it is shockingly bad. Orderly government has ceased to exist. The strike committee suppresses the Press and determines the conditions upon which food, water, gasoline and oil shall be distributed to the citizens, and there is no authority to say it nay, so weak is the spinal column of the constituted authorities. Is there no one to show courage and do the right? Can the crisis produce no man of nerve and fortitude and sense to restore sanity to a people swept from their moorings by Bolsheviks? The Dominion Government is set at defiance by its own officers, sworn guardians of the peace look with kindly eye on the prostration of municipal authority; and a pious prayer that the strikers will not run into excess, and that time will bring a remedy seems the only recourse of those clothed with responsibility. It will all pass away and be forgotten, of course; the sympathetic strikers will weary of their holiday and yearn for the pay envelope, sanity will once more have sway. If these things are not to be, then governments, municipal, provincial and federal, may as well abdicate their functions and confess their incapacity; [sic] since Canada will cease to be a democratic country in which law and order are maintained, the rights of property upheld and personal liberty protected.

---

17 THE ATTEMPTED SUPPRESSION OF THE PRESS

The Manitoba Free Press, Winnipeg
May 22, 1919

The forced suspension of the Free Press was not a part of the general movement to block the varied industrial activities of the city as a supposed protest against the failure of the Metal Trades council to come to terms with the employing iron-masters.

This, of course, is the general opinion of the public, including ninety-five per cent of the members of the organized labor unions themselves. Their view is that the Free Press, like plenty of other innocent businesses, was caught in a storm, and that the resulting damage, while regrettable was an inevitable incident of the general disturbance.

This is an entire misconception. The Free Press WAS NOT THE VICTIM OF "THE GENERAL STRIKE" movement.

Nor was the Free Press sacrificed for the purpose of vindicating the right to "collective bargaining" by the worker – A PRINCIPLE WHICH IS NOT IN QUESTION WITH THE FREE PRESS EITHER IN THEORY OR PRACTICE.

No, the Free Press was the POLITICAL VICTIM of the soviet government. It was "suppressed" by a ukase from the revolutionary head centre because they did not like its views and feared its influence AT THE MOMENT WHEN THEY WERE ATTEMPTING REVOLUTION. They recognized it as an obstacle to the success of the revolution; and they accordingly removed it by an arbitrary and illegal application of force.

All this is in keeping with the doctrines and practices of Lenin and Trotsky, the High Priests of the Winnipeg Reds who were responsible for this conspiracy.

This statement that the Free Press was destroyed as part of a revolutionary movement involving, among other things, the abrogation of the freedom of the press, will strike most people – including all that vast preponderating majority of workers who are not infected with anarchistic ideas – as incredible.

However, this IS NOT A MATTER OF GUESS, or of surmise or of supposition. We have it on the authority of the Strike Committee itself. From the "Special Strike Edition No. 2" of the Western Labor News, published by the Strike Committee, Labor Temple, Monday, May 19 – these are the official titles of the sheet – we quote the following editorial statement:

"The Daily Press.

"For the first time in history, Winnipeg is without its daily press. The reason is clear. It set out once again deliberately to misrepresent the cause of the workers. A year ago we issued a strike bulletin to call their bluff and correct their misstatements. They soon forgot, and again told half-truths or half-suppressed the real facts. Because of this the decree went forth from the Strike Committee that they must be closed.

"We do not think they like it at all, but then, for nearly five years they have been howling their heads off to suppress papers that told the truth – surely it is a case of simple justice at this time to muzzle for a few days the enemies of freedom and truth."

JUST READ THAT OVER AGAIN
AND TAKE IN ITS FULL
MEANING.

The Strike Committee – a mere euphemism this for the dictatorship of our local Lenin and Trotsky – decreed that the Free Press must be closed because they were not satisfied with its editorial conduct.

No doubt these four or five revolutionaries do heartily dislike the Free Press. But there are eighty thousand people in Western Canada who are sufficiently satisfied with the Free Press to pay their good money for the pleasure of reading it. They are the people who have a right to say whether this paper shall continue publication or not.

The right of these eighty thousand persons to say what they shall read in the way of a daily newspaper is brushed aside by the Revolutionary tribunal who undertake to make a decision for them. SO ONE OF THE FIRST ACHIEVEMENTS OF THE NEW REGIME IS TO SUPPRESS THE FREEDOM OF THE PRESS! An auspicious opening for the new era!

But the inspired statement by the Reds shows that other considerations than dislike of the Free Press' attitude towards the inauguration of the soviet regime entered into their action.

There was, in addition, THE MOTIVE OF REVENGE.

FOR WHAT?

For the course which the Free Press took during the war. Please note carefully the language of the statement:

"For nearly five years they have been howling their heads off to suppress papers that told the truth. Surely it is a case of simple justice at this time to muzzle for a few days the enemies of freedom and truth."

There is no doubt about what those words mean.

The five years during which the Free Press and other papers have been persecuting "papers that told the truth" are the five years covering the Great War.

The papers whose woes were so keenly felt by our local galaxy of Reds, were the treasonable pro-German papers published in Canada and the still more dangerous sheets devoted to German propaganda which came in from outside.

These were the only newspapers that were disturbed or suppressed during the war. These are the papers that in the opinion of our soviet governors "told the truth" during the five years when the Free Press was making itself obnoxious to them by its ardent, vigorous, unceasing advocacy of the relentless prosecution of the war to final and complete victory.

Now, by an illegal usurpation of power, in defiance of the laws of the land, in contempt for that liberty which has been our pride, this pestilential brood of anarchists, rankling with the sense of their failure to destroy or limit the participation of Canada in the war, have revenged themselves and their chums and allies, the pacifist, pro-German press, upon one of the agencies that blocked their plans and powerfully assisted in hardening the resolution of the Canadian people to see the thing through.

The Free Press has had to make many sacrifices for the uncompromising course which it followed during the war. This is merely the latest; it makes it gladly and proudly – all the more so as this time it is associated with one of the fundamental necessities of a modern state: Liberty of opinion and a free press.

The Free Press submits its case against these vain and foolish tyrants of an hour to the judgment of free people who know what liberty is and have no intention of exchanging their birthright for revolutionary nostrums imported from Moscow.

---

18 DO NOT USE BLACK PAINT

The Star, Toronto
May 23, 1919

It is satisfying to learn that the issue of dictation or usurpation of power by strikers is disappearing from the Winnipeg situation. It is likely that the opponents of the strikers were unduly sensitive on this point, having in view what has happened in Russia; but it was wise to withdraw the permit signs if they were likely to be misunderstood. The strikers say they were intended merely to protect those members of the unions who by permission remained at work, and so to facilitate the distribution of milk, bread, and other necessaries and prevent hardship. But with so much talk of Soviet and Bolshevism in the air it is well to avoid even the appearance of evil.

It is becoming more and more clear that the issue is not Bolshevism or any attempt to usurp the government of Canada, but a dispute between employers and employed on the questions of wages, hours, recognition of unions, and collective bargaining. A strike covering a wide range of industries of course causes great public inconvenience. But what is the remedy? If it is lawful for one set of workers to strike shall it be made unlawful for two or a dozen to strike? The difference of course is that when a strike is general or of very wide range the matter becomes one of national importance, and the Dominion Government may be warranted and even in duty bound to take strong measures to effect a settlement.

Those employers who hold out against collective bargaining – that is, negotiating with unions which have members working in various establishments – are clearly wrong, and their position cannot be maintained. Collective bargaining is the inevitable result of the modern concentration of industry, and to oppose it is just as extreme as to propose the abolition of organized capital. The organization of labor and the organization of capital are the hard facts of the situation, and must be recognized.

The conflict is of course unfortunate, and we all hope that a settlement may be effected as soon as possible. At the same time nothing is to be gained by exaggerating the evil, painting the situation black, and making Winnipeg look like Petrograd. As a matter of fact, a great deal of restraint and good temper have been shown, and the people of Winnipeg are entitled to credit for their conduct in a trying situation.

Bolshevism is not wanted in Canada, but the name should not be fastened upon labor men who repudiate it. In the early history of this country advocates of responsible government were called rebels, and the temper of moderate reformers must have been sorely tried by the unjust reproach. Let not the mistake be repeated in these days when responsible government in industry has become a practical problem demanding solution.

19 A CHEERFUL LIAR

The Bulletin, Edmonton
May 24, 1919

A Vancouver Province dispatch of May 20th, reports that on Mayor Gray of Winnipeg being interviewed by a deputation of large property owners regarding the strike situation, he declared:

"The citizens need not worry. The situation is well in hand."

The mayor continued: "Law and order have been maintained. Law and order will be maintained at all costs. If any radical element attempts to interfere with enforcement of law and order, we are prepared to smash it immediately. The mayor is directing affairs from his office in the City hall, and the British flag is flying over the building."

Mayor Gray is certainly a cheerful liar. As an unconscious humorist he has them all lashed to the mast. The citizens whose money cannot buy food, or fuel, or clothing, or gasoline, or even milk; or who having these articles for sale cannot sell them, unless permitted to do so by the Soviet government of the city "need not worry." Of course not. All they have to do is to go hungry, or bankrupt, or both. As long as they are willing to submit to these conditions law and order will be maintained, according to Mayor Gray.

By order of the Soviet the water supply of the city is restricted so that houses or buildings of more than two storeys are practically uninhabitable; the street car service has been stopped, the telephone is out of business, the telegraph does not work, and the mails are not carried. It is the place of Mayor Gray, vested with authority as chief magistrate of the city, to provide for the protection of the rights of the citizens in the use of these services. Does he do it? He does not. Are the citizens entitled to these services? They are. If Mayor Gray took active measures to affirm the right of the citizens to those services, would law and order be maintained? He knows that the rights of the citizens could not be secured because of Soviet violence.

It is because the citizens at large under Mayor Gray's direction, have abjectly surrendered to the rule of the Soviet that there has been no interference with the "enforcement of law." But it is Soviet, not city law, that is being enforced.

With such a mayor it is no wonder that Winnipeg is in the condition in which it is today. Citizens generally must realize that they cannot afford to place their civic affairs in the hands of men who have no proper sense of the responsibilities they have assumed.

The climax of the mayor's reply to the deputation is a gem. "The mayor is directing affairs from his office in the City hall, and the British flag is flying over the building." The mayor may be occupying his office in the City hall, but he cannot get a message carried across the street unless the Soviet permits it. As to his reference to the British flag: It has flown for many generations in many corners of the earth and under many varying circumstances; but it is safe to say that it never flew over a more discreditable situation or a more contemptible misrepresentative of civic authority than the present mayor of Winnipeg.

---

20 SUBVERSION DISGUISED AS A STRIKE

The Winnipeg Citizen
May 24, 1919

"It is up to the citizens of Winnipeg to stand firm and resist the efforts made here to overturn proper authority."

This statement was made yesterday by Hon. Arthur Meighen, minister of the interior, who with Senator, the Hon. Gideon D. Robertson, minister of labor, is in the city in connection with the strike situation. The two ministers have let it be know, authoratively [*sic*], that they regard the so-called general strike as a cloak for something far deeper – a cloak for an effort to "overturn proper authority."

The same spirit, they say, has been noticeable in other parts of Canada, and Winnipeg seems to have been chosen as the starting point of the campaign. This is a statement of the views of the two ministers as expressed by themselves.

They stated the opinion that there was a distinct underlying movement beneath the general strike, and that it was this underlying movement, cloaked in the guise of a strike, that they were most concerned about. They designate it as a movement to interfere with or overturn proper governmental authority.

"There is absolutely no justification for the general strike called by the strike committee in this city," said Hon. Arthur Meig-

hen; "there is no right or reason in it, just because three employers and their employes were unable to agree, that a condition should be brought about that imposed hardship upon the whole community."

Mr. Meighen said that it was possible that the ultimate control was altogether outside of the city – that the properties in which the original dispute took place, might be owned by people a thousand miles away. The minister also said that the postal workers had absolutely no reason to strike, as it was only 30 days ago that a delegation of this body waited on the government and went away perfectly satisfied, since the government gave them a hundred dollar bonus more than they asked for, and guaranteed that when the pay-increases came into being they would be retroactive as far back as April 1. When the postal committee left the capital, they thanked the minister for the manner in which they and their demands had been received.

Senator Robertson stated the fact that he had settled the civic strike here last year and that this year schedules were agreed upon between the city and its workers, and signed up. These constituted a solemn and binding contract, said the senator, and the ink was not dry upon it before the civic workers had broken it and walked out.

"No honorable man would endorse the action of the civic employes for one moment," said the senator, in an address to the strike committee yesterday.

The senator stated that postal employes were getting $1,419 per annum each, with clothing, three weeks' holiday on pay, pay when sick, etc., and their increases would go back to April 1. He gave them until Monday at 12:30 to get back to work or have their places probably filled by new and permanent employes. In the meantime he had a hundred volunteers, starting last night at 6 o'clock, to occupy the post office and sort mails until 12:30 Monday.

The postal workers were to have given the senator an answer late yesterday afternoon, but failed to do so.

"There was no justification for the general strike at all," the senator avowed, "and further, the metal trades employes were utterly unjustified in demanding the recognition of councils of unions, such as the Metal Trades Council. They were justified only in asking recognition of craft unions – which were already recognized by their employers. The right of collective bargaining was inalienable, but the collective bargaining was not justifiable through councils or combinations of unions."

There was something underlying this condition in Winnipeg, far deeper than a mere strike. The strike was a cloak for efforts to overturn proper governmental authority.

The kind of collective bargaining, through centralized control like trades councils – or like the One Big Union – demanded by the Trades Council, was utterly unjustified.

21 THE FAILURE OF THE AUTHORITIES

The Manitoba Free Press, Winnipeg
May 24, 1919

The public undoubtedly feels that matters reached the pass they did in this city because the constituted authorities did not challenge the spirit of rebellion the moment it showed itself.

The Dominion Government is now taking action in keeping with its duty but for a whole week it displayed a shocking absence of backbone which did much to encourage the Reds in thinking that they could do as they pleased.

One of the most immediate results of the strike was the stopping of mails for Winnipeg; and not until yesterday was there any action by the authorities to right this intolerable state of affairs.

It must be assumed that when, on Thursday of last week, the mail for Winnipeg was stopped the fact was immediately reported to Ottawa. Did not the Postmaster-General and the acting premier recognize this stopping of His Majesty's mails as an act of war against the sovereignty of the Canadian government? If they did so recognize it why did they lie down under the affront?

There was no business half as important as this before the Dominion Government or the Dominion Parliament. The Government should have taken the position that when trains ran into Winnipeg they must carry the mails intended for this city. If any mail clerk declined to handle the Winnipeg mail he should have been taken off the train and landed in jail and the power of the Government exerted to the extent of replacing him by someone who has prepared to obey the law. When the mail reached Winnipeg it should have been transported to the Post Office if necessary under the charge of the military.

Instead of this direct straightforward understandable course the Post Office Department quit cold. It allowed mail cars to run to Winnipeg without the Winnipeg mails which were dumped off at points east, west and south. It allowed mail clerks to practice discrimination against this city in the discharge of their sworn duties. And it closed up the Winnipeg Post Office – thereby giving the Bolshevists visible and striking evidence, as they thought, of the success of their revolutionary movement.

The dissatisfaction with the course followed by the City Council is widespread and profound. The strike committee now seeks to justify its illegal assumptions of authority by pleading that the city council was a consenting party. It is a fact that the city truckled to the soviet committee in the most abject and humiliating manner. As for the position of our police force, there never has been anything like it outside the realms of opera bouffle [sic]. It is the cold, hard fact that the real allegiance of the force for the past ten days has been to the Strike Committee which was engaged in an anti-social and unlawful campaign against the well-being of the city. The Strike Committee still boasts of its condescension in permitting the force to remain under the nominal direction of the Chief Magistrate.

The Provincial Government was the first to awake to the necessity of offering resistance to the pretensions of the Strike Committee; but it, too, lost an opportunity to challenge the spirit of lawlessness at its first manifestation. It temporized in certain respects when it should have acted vigorously and decisively. The darkened power-house at the Court House and the closed elevators in the public buildings were just so many admissions, while these conditions lasted, that the Government of this Province was at the mercy of the revolutionary junta on James Street. Was it any wonder that their Strike Bulletin should say in jesting earnestness that the new parliament buildings would make a good Labor Temple.

There are some things that simply should not be tolerated. They should be challenged whatever the cost. Defiance of constituted authority is in this class. It should be dealt with the moment it appears. Whatever the odds at the moment there need never be any doubt of the issue. The powers behind authority in this country are overwhelming and can be very speedily massed. A peremptory challenge to the pretensions of the Bolshevists at the very outset of their performance would have been a kindness to them for it would have prevented them from developing the hallucination of their invincibility.

Instead, owing to the obvious unreadiness of the three governments to enter the lists against them, they really came to think that they were about to succeed beyond their wildest expectations. For several days they were enhanced with the vision of the spoil when they came to divide the country among themselves and their following. And now the rosy vision has faded. Before them is Failure, hopeless and complete; and beyond that Reckoning and Retribution.

---

22 FRANTIC PATRIOTISM

Western Labor News, Winnipeg
May 24, 1919

When you have nothing to say; [*sic*] just yell. Such was the advice once given to a politician.

When the reciprocity election was on a few years ago, similar advice was given to (the late) Colonel Glen Campbell by the Conservative party. Glen had expressed himself favorably to reciprocity between Canada and the U.S.A., and when the party decided to oppose it, he asked: "What argument shall I use against it?" They [*sic*]

reply was significant, namely: "Don't argue. Flap the flag."

The "Winnipeg Citizen" has come to the flag flapping stage. The strikers are orderly. Their demands are admitted to be reasonable. The Allied governments have declared for them in toto. So there is but one thing to do. Flap the flag. Wear one in your button hole. Call the strikers Bolshevists. It isn't quite clear what a Bolshevist is; so that is a good expression to use. Then too, "Our Institutions" is a good mouth filling word, so it cannot be quoted too often. It is a fine thing to defend "institutions." No one can be found who oppose this; so a "Soviet government" must be discovered by the Citizen – "By permission of the Strike Committee."

These inane vaporings of "The Citizen" are too absurd to merit much attention from thinking people so we shall not waste much time or space on them. But there are two reasons why they ought to be noticed.

The first is that there are a few people who seem to share the frenzy of the self appointed group behind the "Citizen." It is called a Citizens (?) Committee of 1,000 (?) We are prepared to accept the responsibility of saying that it neither represents the citizens, nor is it composed of 1,000 persons. It represents the Greater Winnipeg Board of Trade, and the Manufacturers Association. It represents very few outside these. Its number may be counted any day as the little group leaves the Industrial Bureau. This group of men have SOMETHING TO PROTECT so it creates an imaginary "revolutionary soviet" as its straw man; and then sets to work to overthrow it by calling citizens meetings and church gatherings to form a volunteer militia.

Not One Case of Disorder

They cannot point to a single case of disorder. This in spite of the fact that over 30,000 persons have been on strike for a week; and in spite of the fact that provocative moves have been made for the express purpose of bringing the thing to a head by causing trouble; and still further, in spite of the publication of "The Citizen" filled daily with the bitterest venom and innuendo – without permission of the strike committee

– We say, in spite of these things, they have not been able to incite one single case of disorder, so at their meetings, held for recruiting, the speakers "have information which they are not at liberty to divulge" that would prove the immediate necessity of having an adequate militia.

At this point we respectfully draw the attention of the "The Citizen" to the fact that the only disorder in this city at this time is in the brains of the group behind its own vaporings. We agree that in that direction there is much disorder, and, as a consequence, we understand clearly why they "are not at liberty to divulge the nature of the information" they have.

---

23   WE MUST GO FORWARD

Western Labor News, Winnipeg
May 24, 1919

We are engaged today in a struggle, the immediate cause of which is well known to all. Long and bitter experience has taught us that in order to maintain a family in common decency, we must develop some power greater than our individual ability to persuade our masters to grant us a living wage.

How many of us know however, what a price has been paid by our progenitors in order to leave us some semblance of decency and freedom? How many of us know of the struggle, the degradation, the blood and the tears that have been the lot of the working class throughout the ages? They appealed in their ignorance to the hearts of their oppressors, only to find that they were men of stone. They cried unto the heavens for aid believing their cause to be a righteous one, but the great silence only mocked them in their misery. They pointed out the justice of their cause, only to discover that the conceptions of justice held by master and slave could never coincide. Every forward step they have made has been secured only when the ruling class has no longer deemed it safe to refuse it.

This must be the case in any society where it is the function of one class to exploit another. This fact has slowly forced itself upon the minds of the workers, and in order to continue their existence, they were compelled to organize, to band themselves into groups for the purpose of resisting the oppression to which they were subjected as individuals.

This spirit of co-operation, quite naturally used the craft as the basis for organization, but, with the development of machinery, and the elimination of the craftsmans skill, the basis of organization broadens to meet the new conditions. Those who demand that we revert back to an obsolete method of organization and refuse to recognize or to negotiate with the new, but reveal their inability to grasp the logic of modern development.

We have a historical mission to perform. We have no choice but to go forward. Our basis of organization must broaden still further, and develop until it embraces all who perform a useful function in society; until it eliminates the wages system with all its resultant evils of wealth and poverty, and establishes in its stead a system where usefulness and not profit will be the basis of production.

---

24   MUZZLING THE WINNIPEG PRESS

The Whig, Kingston
May 26, 1919

The action which did most harm to the cause of the strikers in Winnipeg was the muzzling of the public press. The executive of the strikers' organization explained that it was necessary at this time to muzzle for a few days the enemies of freedom and truth. This explanation has led some of the thinking people to at once conclude that the cause of the strikers was a weak one, and collapse soon followed.

Those men who are in touch with public affairs are naturally amazed at this attitude of the striking element. The public press has, with a very few exceptions, always been found on the side of truth and freedom. The freedom of the press is one of the most valuable and jealously guarded institutions of the British Empire. The press has always fought consistently for the liberty and freedom of the people. The press has always been the first to espouse and support any righteous or just cause. The press is the only channel through which the strikers could have made their case known to the public and through which they could have gained that very essential factor, public sympathy. But they had the mistaken idea that they could ride roughshod over the rest of the populace, and the result was failure.

This failure was largely the result of the muzzling of the newspapers of Winnipeg. Had the cause of the strikers been a just one, they would have found no stronger supporters than the press. Canada has been fortunate in that its newspapers are inspired by motives of the highest type. Patriotism is dominant, but it is tempered with a determination to ensure that the people of our nation shall have everything that is necessary to their comfort and well-being. Any movement which is for the betterment of living and working conditions will always meet with approval and support. The strikers claimed that their movement was for such a purpose, but they closed up their most efficient mouthpiece. The result should be a lesson that the press of Canada must be free and untrammeled, that it must bow to the wishes of no party, and that it must be kept as it is now, the moulder of public opinion and the mouthpiece of all causes which are worthy and just.

25 THE STRIKE AND ITS LESSONS

The Guardian, Charlottetown
May 26, 1919

The recent strike in Winnipeg, now, we trust, over, has taught a number of lessons which it is hoped will not be overlooked or forgotten. The right of labor to strike for the redress of a real grievance, after all other expedients have failed, is admitted by all, and no fault will be found with it by Canadians. It is labor's only defence against any form of injustice.

The right of nine unions out of ten to strike in sympathy with the tenth requires adjustment. The nine may be perfectly satisfied with their wages and with all the attendant conditions; the tenth may have a real grievance and, because of that grievance involving a few score of men, the other nine, involving thousands of men and their families and involving also the whole commercial, industrial and social life of a city, as was the case in Winnipeg, are called out on strike. True, this is where the power of the Union lies, yet in view of the widespread injustice to those who are carrying on their work to the mutual satisfaction of themselves, their employers and the general public, the line at which such asympathetic strike may be justifiable, should be re-examined and re-set by legislation.

This however, is not the greatest problem. Canadian labor, like British labor, if left to itself, may be depended upon to act sanely in any kind of crisis. It may insist upon its rights to the point of striking or fighting if necessary, but it will demand only its rights and will not unnecessarily inflict injustice upon the innocent. The real danger is when it falls under the spell of the agitator, the alien enemy, the Bolshevik and it is now known pretty definitely that this is what happened in Winnipeg. The attempt to obtain Soviet control of the civic government to isolate the city from the outside world, and to disorganize all civic and social activities was of foreign origin, engineered by enemy agitators whose sole object was to plunge the whole country into revolution and bloodshed. And if bloodshed had come these loudmouthed agitators would not have been found in the front ranks. They would have been across the border at the sound of the first gunfire.

It is very apparent now that the Canadian Labor Unions involved in the Winnipeg strike were made a catspaw for foreign agitators and enemies and the Unions have found it out. There are enough foreigners among the rank and file of laborers in Winnipeg to keep the agitation at white heat and the only hope for Canadian Unionism today is to expel every foreigner who mouths anarchy. Sedition is punishable by death and the penalty should be exacted to the full whenever it shows itself.

26 ABDICATING GOVERNMENT

The Gazette, Montreal
May 26, 1919

This editorial was reprinted two days later, without acknowledgement, by the Fredericton *Gleaner*, as representative of its own opinion.

The two Federal Ministers who proceeded to Winnipeg to pour oil upon the troubled waters have plucked up courage enough to notify the striking postal clerks that unless they resume their duties at noon today their services will not thereafter be employed. That ultimatum should have been issued within twenty-four hours of the time these officials walked out, and no other word than pusillanimity adequately describes the failure of the Government to promptly and vigorously cope with the Winnipeg situation in respect of officials of the Crown. It may well be doubted whether the people of Canada have grasped the gravity of the plight to which Government has been reduced. Parliament, the Ministry, are openly flouted by their servants, who violate their oaths of office, and bring the business of the third largest city in Canada almost to a standstill, literally isolating it from the outside world, so far as the mails are concerned, and for eleven days the Federal authorities look helplessly on. Surely something is rotten in the State of Denmark, or would it be unfair to paraphrase Shylock's words and say of Parliament:

"Still have we borne it with a patient shrug,
"For office is the greed of all our tribe."

The case of the postal clerks, or of any other public officers, is essentially different from that of men in private employment. These officers have taken oath to perform their duties, and are given permanent tenure of place, subject to good behavior. The constitutional law is that they may remain in undisturbed possession of their offices so long as they continue to discharge their functions properly. Engaging in party politics while capably performing official duties is made a misdemeanor punishable by dismissal, but total abnegation of those duties, abstention from work by deliberate, organized, conspiracy, becomes a venial offence to be pardoned if the striking officials will graciously consent to resume their occupation. Parliament is in session; yet not a voice of protest comes from any member, so fearful and spineless are these representatives of the people. Where is that sovereign Law we boast as the bulwark of order and established government? If the postal clerks of Winnipeg can at their own sweet will abandon their posts, so can the postal clerks the country over; and not alone the postal clerks, but customs officers and employees in every branch of the public service. To tolerate the conduct of the Winnipeg officials is to destroy the very foundation of government, to make impotent the power of cabinet and Parliament and to put the Soviet in the saddle where popular government now sits. And if it be said that the people rule, and must have their sway, the ready rejoinder is that the people of Canada have not yet shown themselves so bereft of sense as to desire that the administration of their public affairs shall be carried on by means of a strike as the alternative of collective bargaining. The matter penetrates into the very marrow of our constitutional system of government.

What the Government should have done, what the Government may yet be required to do, is to dispense with the services of the postal clerks at Winnipeg, who have voluntarily relinquished their duties, suspend the Civil Service Act and fill the vacancies as rapidly as possible with men who will regard their oath and responsibilities. As the Duke of Wellington once remarked, "the Queen's Government must be carried on." Government has not been carried on in Winnipeg for ten days. An important branch of the service, intimately related to the social and business life of the community, has broken down, without immediate effort to repair it. There were no grievances to redress that were not in course of adjustment, or that could not be adjusted by the people – the employers of these officers – through the Cabinet or Parliament; and if the public service of Canada is to be regulated by the device of strikes, sympathetic or otherwise, the sooner the people learn where they are at, the better. No question of more transcendent importance can be faced.

---

27 LABOUR WILL NEVER GIVE UP

Western Labor News, Winnipeg
May 27, 1919

"THE ISSUE – A NEW PHASE"

The issue of the general strike from the standpoint of the workers is clear.

They Demand: –
  (1) The Right of Collective Bargaining.
  (2) A Living Wage.

Their Demands are Just:-

Their demands are established in the laws of the nations as signed at the peace treaty.

Men everywhere say there can be no fault found with these demands. But

The Committee of 1000 Demands:- That,
  (1) The General Strike must be called off.
  (2) Policemen's, Firemen's, Postal, Waterworks, City Light and Power, and Telephone unions be declared illegal if they affiliate with each other or with any other bodies.

This Creates a New Issue.

The ramifications of the demands of the committee of 1,000 are far reaching. If they were granted the backbone of the principle of organized labor would be broken.

The things they ask mean that:-

1. No union shall at any time, under any circumstances, or for any purpose, strike in sympathy with another craft.

2. No union on public utilities shall affiliate with any other public utility or with any national, or international labor movement.

3. The result would be that labor would become impotent in the face of an almost omnipotent aggregation of financial interests.

4. It would turn the clock back for the labor movement by twenty years.

The committee of 1,000 knows this and so makes its demands.

A Specious Plea

These men put up a specious plea, and at the same time they play upon the passions of the people.

These arguments are:-

I. The General Strike is undemocratic and it makes the innocent suffer with the guilty.

(This has a wide application in life, but they apply it only to the General Strike. It suits their purpose so to do).

II. The General Strike is part of a plot to overthrow the constitution.

(They use the efforts of the workers in the direction of forming a more effective industrial organization, under the name of One Big Union, as the basis of their argument. They do this in spite of the fact that they know the forward industrial movement is inevitable and entirely constitutional).

III. The agitation is the work of the alien.

(Just why there is unrest in every nation they do not say. But they are sure that the alien is the cause of the troubles here.

As we see it, this is their clever trick to draw attention from themselves and their profiteering. If they do not attack somebody, then somebody else will attack them.

There were members of their own class who acknowledged while the Mathers Commission sat in Winnipeg that the High Cost of Living is the cause of the unrest. But they forget that today. The cause of the unrest has changed during the last two weeks, and today it is the alien who is at the bottom of it all.)

IV. Their last argument is that the General Strike was engineered by Five Men. Five red men. Some of these have English names such as Robinson – but this is merely a corruption of Rubenstein – so, though Robinson is English born, he must be a Jew. Ivens – yes, yes, that sounds like Ivan – so he must be Russian – "Ivens the Terrible", is an excellent rendition of his name. Veitch – Veitch – where can that come from, ah – got it – he must be Bukowinian. Winning –

Winning – they stick on Winning – They must not talk about that name. The strikers must not win – they must not even think they are winning, so his name is passed up. Russell – Russel [sic] is easy – The first letter gets him. R – R – R he must be Scotch.

Thus, by an analysis of names the Red Five are the leaders of the strike.

V. The Solution.

Deport the five. "The rosy vision has faded. Before them is failure, hopeless and complete; and, beyond that, Reckoning and Retribution.

VI. The Reply of Labor is Clear.

1. Labor will never give up its right to strike in the support of its fellows.

2. Every worker is a worker on public utility. All real work is necessary for the whole community.

Therefore every worker in every industry and undertaking must have the same rights of organization.

3. Labor will go forward to greater and still greater effectiveness of organization. Those who work must determine the conditions of their work.

The future must increase the power of the worker in the control of industry; and the ultimate goal is the ownership of the tools of production by the workers, the control of the industry by the workers, and the distribution of the product of industry on the most equitable basis for all the people – who would then be workers.

4. The workers are not led by irresponsible men. They are not lead at all in the generally understood sense of the word. The independence of the worker is being demonstrated in his union as well as in the shops. The rank and file dictate the policy. The most the leaders can do is to voice the sentiments of the whole body.

5. Labor will stand shoulder to shoulder to gain the two principles upon which the strike is called. It is a fight to a finish. The right to collective bargaining and to a living wage must be established once and for all. Until Winnipeg Labor won this right the General Strike must continue. The next step is to call for the help of every organized worker to back this demand.

6. The whole Dominion will be called out by gradual steps till our cause is won.

---

28 THE NAKED FACT OF REVOLUTION

The Winnipeg Citizen
May 27, 1919

No thoughtful citizen can any longer doubt that the so-called general strike is in reality revolution – or a daring attempt to overthrow the present industrial and governmental system.

If any serious-minded trades unionist who was betrayed into a wholly illegal and unjustified strike, had any doubt that the so-called strike was something of far deeper and of sinister moment, surely he must have been startled into a realization of what is afoot, by the open and rebellious defiance of the Governments of Canada and of Manitoba respectively.

The Dominion Government ordered its postal employes to return to the [sic] duties – their sworn duties – by yesterday at noon, under pain of dismissal from their positions. What was the answer? – The answer was an absolute defiance and challenge to the authority of the Government, an authority which the federal ministry is bound to vindicate.

The Manitoba Government, through its telephone commissioner, ordered the striking Manitoba Government Telephones Employes back to work by Monday at noon, under pain of dismissal from their positions – and the answer, as in the case of the postal employes, was a flat defiance of the authority of the Provincial Government.

Coupled with these two instances of rebellion we find the expression of defiance amplified in the Labor News with the following words:

"The Committee of A Thousand has at last secured the backing of the various authorities to the extent that they are now issuing ultimatums that they" (presumably the strikers) "return to work at once or be dismissed permanently... Labor will accept the challenge of the financial giants of today. It, too, will fight to a finish. Instead of this struggle nearing its end, it has only just sounded the first bugle-call to muster its forces. A FEW DAYS MORE AND EVERY WHEEL IN THE DOMINION WILL STOP. Another week will see it Dominion-wide unless the bosses yield."

Particularly note that according to the self-styled dictator of Winnipeg who edits the Labor News, this is "the first bugle call of Labor to muster its forces." This is an absolute vindication, coupled with current events, of the statement made by The Citizen yesterday, that the Winnipeg "strike" is the first concrete overt act of the "One Big Union" revolutionary campaign.

29 IS THE STRIKE "REVOLUTIONARY"?

The World, Vancouver
May 27, 1919

It is easy to say that the Winnipeg strike is a determined attempt to "overthrow constitutional government in Canada." But the statement is an exaggeration and a misrepresentation.

Not even the bitterest revolutionary Socialist in the Dominion would attempt anything of the sort at this juncture. For one reason he could hope to effect his purpose only through the existing labor unions of Canada which, all told, have a membership amounting only to a fraction of the adult male population of the Dominion. For another the conservative element in the labor ranks has no such end in view. And, furthermore, the returned soldiers who have joined the labor ranks would be the last persons in Canada to countenance seditious activity.

The Winnipeg strike and those declared in sympathy with it may be regarded rather as a demonstration of the growing strength of the labor movement and as evidence of the increasing determination of the leaders of that movement to secure a better livelihood for the workingman. No doubt there are extremists in the movement as there are in every movement, but in general the cause of labor unrest is not an irresponsible spirit of revolution but a widespread discontent with present conditions, discontent with the economic pressure which at times bears so heavily on the industrial class, together with a strongly-stimulated sense of social injustice.

If instead of denouncing every labor outbreak as "revolutionary" and "disloyal" an attempt was made to understand the reasons behind it, the causes which induce workingmen to act as they do, something might be accomplished toward permanent settlement. There is in the labor movement, a strongly conservative element which, we are convinced, would respond to reasonable overtures from employers and public. But if those overtures are not made and things are allowed to drift as they have been drifting, the present state of armed peace which from time to time bursts into industrial warfare as in Winnipeg, must lead to an explosion sooner or later.

This Dominion is passing through a labor crisis such as a more highly industrialized country like Great Britain has already experienced. In Britain the crisis was met by a wide extension of the economic control of industry by the workers, by the creation of a Labor Party in Parliament able to influence directly all forms of legislation, and by national approval of the principle of self-government of industry.

30 EXTREMISTS ON BOTH SIDES

The Star, Toronto
May 27, 1919

Dealing With the Extremists

The Dominion Ministers now in Winnipeg, Senator Robertson and Mr. Meighen, seem to have come to the conclusion that the Winnipeg strike is a cloak for a conspiracy to overturn authority. If they have evidence of such a conspiracy it is of course their duty to defeat it. Their duty, however, is not fully discharged by an order that employes of the Government shall return to work. It is certain that a very large number of workers, probably the majority, entertained no idea of subverting authority or forcibly changing the form of government, but were on strike simply for better conditions of labor and the recognition of unions.

All the extremists were not on one side. Those employers who obstinately refused to admit the principle of collective bargaining must bear a large share of the blame. The *Citizen*, representing the opponents of the strikers, says that the remedy for the evil is the open shop, that is, a declaration of war upon the unions. We have no hesitation in saying that the remedy lies in exactly the opposite direction – that is, in a frank and cheerful recognition of unionism, organized labor, and collective bargaining.

This is the conclusion which has been arrived at in Great Britain, where there is an immensely larger fund of experience in regard to industrial conditions and disputes than there is in Canada, and where the subject has all through the war been a subject of anxious study. The sweeping condemnation of unionism and the attempt to identify it with Bolshevism are unwise. In the same manner attempts have been made in the past to check political reform by branding the reformers as rebels.

Having asserted the authority of the Government it is to be hoped that the Minister of Labor and Mr. Meighen will use their influence for the purpose of obtaining a just settlement of all the questions involved in the Winnipeg strike. The Government, by appointing a commission to enquire into industrial relations, recognizes that present conditions are not satisfactory, and the whole Winnipeg situation should be carefully studied with the purpose of improving those conditions.

31 COLLECTIVE BARGAINING

The Herald, Hamilton
May 27, 1919

One of the demands made by the Winnipeg strike committee is recognition by the employers of the principle of collective bargaining. The Winnipeg employers endorse the principle and agree to act upon it.

But the strike committee's notion of collective bargaining differs from the employers' notion; and it is not likely that the two interpretations can be reconciled.

Collective bargaining, according to the common acceptation of the term, is negotiation between the employers in a particular industry and chosen workers representing the crafts engaged in that industry, with a view of agreeing upon wage scales and working conditions. That is the sort of collective bargaining that the Winnipeg employers will agree to. The strike committee's interpretation is that any agreement arranged by employers and the representatives of workers engaged in any craft must first be submitted to and endorsed by the central labor body before it becomes effective – the central Labor body having the right either to accept or reject the agreement. Such an arrangement would, of course, deprive any union of craft workers of the power to make final agreements with employers.

This form of collective bargaining proposed by the Winnipeg strike committee has been rejected by the committee representing the citizens of Winnipeg. It is also condemned by Senator Robertson, minister of labor, who points out that it would deprive craft workers of a right which they have acquired after a long struggle and which they dearly prize; also that it would concentrate absolute power in the hands of a few irresponsible Labor leaders who might be self-appointed and who would be very likely to abuse their power.

Thus, when it is stated that employers reject the principle of collective bargaining, it is important to know the form of collective bargaining which they reject. It is clear that the form which is demanded by the Winnipeg strike committee is an essential feature of the One Big Union plan, which rejects craft unionism and aims to concentrate power in the hands of a central body exercising dictatorial authority. Such a system is necessary to the effective carrying on of general strikes, and it is by means of the general strike that the One Big Union promoters hope to paralyze industry, bring about widespread distress, and compel the majority of the people, through sheer despair, to turn for relief to the establishment of state socialism or communism or sovietism or some other revolutionary social and industrial system – whichever one may be the most in favor at the time.

---

32 WHY THE GENERAL STRIKE WEAPON

Western Labor News, Winnipeg
May 28, 1919

The workers have never liked to down tools. It means hard times for them. Many never have enough to live on. The strike takes away all their living. For this reason they strike only when they are driven to desperation.

Why then, it will be asked, do unions that have no direct disagreements of their own walk out with others who have a disagreement? Why do they join in a general strike.

Others add the question, why should they put the whole community to a disadvantage because they take up the quarrel of others.

To answer adequately this question would take a volume. But we can indicate the answer.

First, labor will not call a general strike on a question of wages alone. It wants a decent wage, but so far as we know, no general strike was ever called for this reason alone. It is when principles that cannot be arbitrated are involved and would be defeated unless there were a general stand made by labor that a general strike is possible. It is never possible otherwise.

That was the issue in this city a year ago. The right of the firemen and police to organize was challenged, and labor by a very gradual process brought out one union after the other until the unions concerned were recognized.

This year the issue arose over the Metal Trades. The employers here were arrogant and defiant. They threatened to practically close up and the men might starve. Such was the essence of the matter.

In the case of the Building Trades workers it was the matter of wages. But not a mere matter of wages either. Their demands were acknowledged to be fair and reasonable. But the banking interests were behind the scenes, and the employers were not free to pay the reasonable wage. Thus, labor was fact to face with a wage crisis that had never before appeared. It was a straight demand on the part of our financial barons that the workers should work for less than a living wage, while they piled up more millions. That was why the men involved struck work. That is – they just stopped working on those terms.

A couple of weeks sufficed to demonstrate that the employers had determined that they would not run the foundries or erect buildings, and the workers were faced with the alternatives of going on under impossible conditions or calling the whole force of labor to their assistance.

They did the latter. Will those who oppose the general strike say that there was a better way? Will they say that labor had any alternative?

But others suffer besides the original parties, they say. That is true. But, is labor responsible for that? Is it not the financial autocrats and barons who are responsible? The answer is clear. Labor has no choice. Moreover, for thousands of workers to stop work and lose their wages in the interests of others is the highest form of brotherhood. It cannot be condemned. Still further, it is wholly a negative method. It does not consist in destruction or violence, but merely is a cessation of work. It has no other phases. It is wholly a cessation of work.

If the general public is so considerably inconvenienced when labor ceases to work, is it not convincingly clear that it is the business of all the people to see that labor gets such a wage and such working conditions as tend to contentment and efficiency? Yet, when was the public interested in labor? When did they do a tap to help get justice for the worker? To ask is to answer the question.

---

33 A COLLECTIVE BARGAIN SHOULD BE A BARGAIN

The Star, Toronto
May 28, 1919

In a conference held at Winnipeg to bring about a settlement the question of collective bargaining was pretty thoroughly discussed. The term has been used in several ways. There have been employers who refused to negotiate or bargain with any body of workmen except their own employes. This attitude has been abandoned by most employers in Canada and by practically all in Great Britain. The next step is recognition of a craft union, confined to a particular trade. Many employers who have progressed this far think they have gone far enough, and object to the recognition of a body representing a group of trades, such as the Metal Trades Council. Their hesitation may be natural, but we do not see how it is possible to stop short of the principle that workers have a right to appoint the agents by whom their labor is to be sold.

Those who advocate collective bargaining must, we are sure, admit that a bargain once made must be kept. Men who have agreed to work for a certain period on certain conditions should carry out that agreement so long as it is being carried out in good faith by the other party to it. They should not break it merely because men in some other employment are dissatisfied and even have good ground for dissatisfaction. The case of men who are engaged in some public utility and are working under the terms of an award made under the Industrial Disputes Act is not precisely the same, but so nearly the same that we think the same rule should apply. Workmen should regard themselves as bound by an agreement or by an award so long as the obligation is recognized and fulfilled on the other side. To break a bargain is to aim a blow at collective bargaining, and to repudiate an accepted award is to aim a blow at the principle of arbitration and conciliation and the peaceful settlement of disputes.

The formation of groups of unions and the sympathetic strikes are signs of the growing cohesion of the working classes, and the sense that their interests are identical. The sympathetic strike is more likely to come when recognition of unions is refused, because such refusal is felt to be a blow aimed at all labor interests. A dispute over that question is felt to be radically different from one over such details as wages and hours of labor. But on whatever grounds a sympathetic strike is called it ought not to be resorted to by any body of men who are under an agreement to sell their labor for a given time upon certain terms and conditions.

A large body of citizens are [sic] not directly concerned in labor disputes on one side or the other, but are [sic] liable to suffer serious inconvenience or even hardship when a strike is on an extensive scale, especially if it touches a public utility, or some service or commodity that is urgently needed. These people are swayed toward one side or the other by reasonable or unreasonable conduct, and it is a matter of great importance for employers and workers to retain their sympathy. We have known the people of Toronto to be very patient under very serious inconvenience caused by a strike, when they were sure the strikers were right. But they are not disposed to listen to the most ingenious arguments in favor of any extreme course or any theory carried beyond the limits of what they regard as common sense.

It is always wise to take counsel with "the man on the street," the man who has no interest of his own to serve and no particular theory as to industrial relations, but who has a sense of fair play and a desire for goodwill. These men constitute the jury by whom the verdict will be given, and a cause may be wrecked by losing their confidence.

---

34 THE BOLSHEVIKS SHOULD BE DEPORTED

The Leader, Regina
May 28, 1919

THE MOTIVE BEHIND.

In his message to the Mayor of Calgary, printed elsewhere in this issue, Hon. G. D. Robertson, Minister of Labor, says in part:

"Twenty-four hours before the sympathetic strike was called the Premier of Manitoba urged an adjustment of the matters in dispute by arbitration, and, in a final attempt to avert a general strike, asked the committee if they would cancel the strike provided the employers would agree to recognize the Metal Trades Council. To this question a negative reply was given.

"Subsequently, events have proved conclusively that the motive behind the general strike effort was for the purpose of assuming control and direction of industrial affairs, also of municipal, Provincial and Federal activities, so far as they are being carried on in this city, and with the avowed intention of extending that control to a wider field.

"I have no hesitation in saying that the 'One Big Union' movement is the underlying cause of the whole trouble, and that the Winnipeg general strike deserves no sympathy or support from the labor organizations outside Winnipeg."

Thus the Minister of Labor, after a thorough investigation of the situation at Winnipeg, finds that the motive behind the general strike was practically the creation of a Bolshevik dictatorship, for the "control and direction of industrial affairs, also of municipal, provincial and Dominion activities with the avowed intention of extending that control to a wider field" means nothing else. This, of course, would create anarchy, the I. W. W. paradise.

Such an objective and the principles of organized labor are as far apart as the poles, but the promoters of the Winnipeg trouble are trying to divert the trades unionist movement into channels of lawlessness and chaos, to shackle it to the mad ideas of Lenine and Trotzky [sic]. It is not a little surprising that they have been able to deceive and dominate so large a proportion of the organized labor membership of Winnipeg so long. No doubt the big alien element in that membership was an important factor in helping to produce the few days' paralysis, and not improbably it was this circumstance which induced the promoters to select Winnipeg as a strategic battleground.

The revolutionary movement at Winnipeg will fail, no matter how far its ramifications may extend, for the Canadian people will have none of it. But it will have taught certain useful lessons. One is the folly of permitting preachers of disruption and anarchy to enter this country, and of allowing them to carry on their campaign after they come here. Every revolutionary utterance from them is a violation of the law and should be dealt with as such.

Another lesson is the urgency of Government action relative to the cost of living, profiteering, and other economic disabilities from which the country is suffering. The existence of these produces a condition of mind which greatly assists the propagators of discord. But for these the Bolshevik movement in Winnipeg would not have gained any support, no matter how attractively it was garbed, except from the aliens and other agitators who are not aliens but who should be deported to the country from which they came just the same.

35 PUBLIC SERVANTS AND STRIKES

The Post, Sydney, N. S.
May 29, 1919

The Winnipeg strike seems to be slowly but surely heading for a settlement. The "sympathetic" feature is disappearing. Most of the civic employees, and virtually all the striking postal officials, have returned to duty. The statement of Messrs. Meighen and Robertson in Winnipeg, and that of Sir Robert Borden in the House of Commons, that the postal clerks would either have to return to work at once or quit the public service, were followed by a lively scramble of those officials to get back to their posts of duty. The civic government has followed the lead of the Federal authorities, and their announcement that the city's servants must choose forthwith whom they would serve, has had a like effect. It is highly probable that the defection of these bodies from the conspiracy will be effectual in breaking the deadlock, and that a settlement of the differences between the metal workers and their employees will soon be brought about.

Strikes by government officials and the employees of municipal authorities should be prohibited by law. Until the past year, no one dreamed that such a law should be necessary, but the unrest amongst all wage-earners in Canada, in common with those of other countries, which is one of the most notable after-effects of the war, has upset many of the sane conceptions of by-gone days, and resulted in much confusion of thought. One of the old-fashioned ideas which seems to have temporarily gone by the boards, is that a government officer is the servant, not of any capitalist or group of capitalists, but of the public. But the temporary craze for strikes the country is now experiencing, has infected civic officials, sworn to do their duty, and stick to their posts, as well as government officials, who entered the public service under conditions regulating hours of work, scales of remuneration, and rules of promotion, fired by the law of the land. To enter upon a strike for the changing of such conditions is to endeavor to get the law changed by a demonstration of force. For public servants to participate in a strike, as the officials at Winnipeg have done, and to work havoc with the most important of the public services of the community, merely to aid others in their disputes with their employers, is to aim a deliberate blow, without provocation, and without even the poor justification of individual grievances, at the administrative organization of the country, which it is their first duty to maintain at its highest efficiency. For such persons, hardly any discipline the departments concerned might impose, would seem to be too severe. In normal times, men who acted in such a manner, should be summarily dismissed from the public service, and declared permanently incapable of reentering it. But it is fair to remember that these are not normal times, and that there is a kind of insanity abroad, such for example as so often deprives men of their mental perspective, in the frenzy and excitement of a fierce political contest. "The world gone mad," is not an empty phrase, or one that expresses a merely imaginary condition. There are occasions when the steadying forces of reason and reflection are momentarily subordinated, even in the most staid and orderly communities, to the play of passion and fanaticism. Community after community, in Canada and in other civilized countries, has recently given ample evidence of this fact. The time will come when we shall all review, in dispassionate retrospect and amazement, experiences through which we are passing just now.

In all the circumstances, therefore, the Government should not deal with these offending public servants as strictly as the nature of their misdemeanors would appear to warrant. But the excesses committed in Winnipeg should have their lessons for all concerned. They should be an effective object-lesson to the offending officials, of the utter inconsistency of the action of a striker with the duty of a public servant. And they should impress on parliament the necessity of prohibiting by law, under heavy penalties, participation in strikes by the men the country looks to for the carrying on of the public services.

36 A HUN-LIKE DIMINUENDO

The Telegram, Winnipeg
May 30, 1919

The Labor News is becoming so docile and pacific that one can scarcely recognize it as the same sheet produced by the same men that boasted such a short time ago that the revolutionary strike committee had Winnipeg firmly in its grasp, had "muzzled the press" and held all industry, even the distribution of food supply, at its mercy.

Today the Strike Bulletin adopts a whining key. It protests in a tone of injured innocence that the strike ringleaders are not revolutionists at all, that they aim at nothing like revolution, that they are merely devoted men and women, faithfully, constitutionally and modestly striving to obtain for the working classes a living wage and the right of collective bargaining.

One will recall the German attitude towards the opinion of the world before the Battle of the Marne. How it reminds one of the attitude of the Strike Bulletin two weeks ago! Then one will recall the German attitude after the Battle of the Marne. How it reminds one of the present attitude of the Strike Bulletin!

Before the Battle of the Marne, when well-nigh helpless Belgium and Northern France were being trampled in the mud, when every outrage conceivable was being practised openly and without pretence, the Germans boasted that their aim was to dominate the world. After the Battle of the Marne, they adopted the whining tone, and undertook elaborately to convince civilization that poor Germany had no ambition but to wage a defensive war to save the Fatherland from the aggressiveness of envious neighbors.

Before the citizens of Winnipeg awoke to a realization that a revolution was being conducted in this City, the conspirators had things pretty much their own way. This and that was "permitted by order of the Strike Committee." Everything else was "verboten." When Winnipeg awoke, and began to assert her might, the whining tone of the cringing hypocrite was adopted by the ringleaders in all this deplorable mischief. They undertook and still endeavor to convince the outraged people against whom they had conspired and are still conspiring, that their objects are of the most worthy and modest kind. All they seek is "a fair living wage" and "the right of collective bargaining."

Pure hypocritical cant and contemptible duplicity! Today the conspirators fear to admit to those very men and women they have deceived and imposed upon – the men and women whom they have induced by false pretences to strike – that their object was and is revolution, the establishing of a Soviet form of Government, after our honest British system should be overthrown – the erection in this City first, and in Canada after, of Lenine's [sic] regime, with all its disgusting depravity, all its riot of loot, lewdness and lust; all its tyrannical oppression, bloodshed and famine, that a few adventurous mountebanks might enrich themselves at the expense of honest men of brains and industry, who have accumulated some holdings in lands, machinery and cash, which excite the envy of the burglariously inclined.

The vast majority of those citizens of Winnipeg who are now on strike are thoroughly respectable, well intentioned good citizens. They would not knowingly touch so depraved and hideous a thing as Bolshevism any more readily than they would long to fondle some grotesquely shapen prehistoric lizard. They would shrink from it in horror, if they were to be convinced of its true character.

This the little coterie of conspirators fully realize. Consequently they hide as much as possible their real purpose. They talk of "a living wage," as if a living wage were even in dispute. They talk of the "right of collective bargaining," as if that right has been challenged.

How many unions asked for an increase of wages before striking "in sympathy?" Not one! How many unions found their employers unwilling to recognize the right of collective bargaining before they struck "in sympathy?" Not one!

Why, then, this absurd and ridiculous lie, to the effect that this so-called strike is on the purpose of obtaining a living wage or the recognition of a right that is not challenged?

Does any sane man or woman in Winnipeg among the strikers really believe that Senator Robertson, Minister of Labor, and a life-long union man himself, would misinterpret such a thing as the right of collective bargaining? Does any sane man or woman among the strikers really believe for a moment that he does not understand the real situation in Winnipeg, after coming here and making a study of the whole thing, and obtaining all the information that union officials could give him? Surely not!

Yet Senator Robertson has stated that the strike is quite unjustified, that it has not been called for the purpose that the strike ringleaders profess, but that it is a deliberate attempt – a conspiracy – to overthrow the Canadian constitution, and to set up Soviet rule in this City and in this Nation.

Senator Robertson's condemnation alone ought to be sufficient to convince every true Canadian in the strikers' ranks that he or she has been imposed upon in a most heartless manner, and used to serve the purposes of men and women so lost to all sense of decency, patriotism and fair play that their continued presence in Winnipeg has become intolerable.

If any union now out were really on strike to obtain a living wage, The Telegram would be right behind that union. If any union now out were on strike for the purpose of compelling an employer to recognize the right of collective bargaining – which right this newspaper recognizes, both in principle and in practice – The Telegram would be solidly behind that union.

It is because this newspaper knows absolutely that the present strike has been called for no such purpose, but for the purpose of wrecking the finest system of Government that has been evolved in five thousand years of human experience, that it opposes wholeheartedly and without any qualification whatever, to the extreme limit of its ability and power, every phase and aspect of this monstrous folly.

The strike is breaking and rapidly coming to an end. But it will have come to an unsatisfactory end, if it should not end with the conviction firmly implanted in the mind of every loyal striker, who has been deceived, that he or she has been deceived, and that he or she has no worse enemy than those who conspired to use him or her as a tool to advance an enterprise that is at once loathsome, bloody and lewd – an enterprise that could not succeed without imposing upon us all the horrors that have made Russia a wilderness and set it back a generation on the road to comfort and content.

37 AN AMERICAN VIEWPOINT

The New York Evening Globe
May 30, 1919

TROUBLE IN CANADA

With a general strike going into effect at Toronto today, the situation in Canada becomes decidedly more serious. Already half a dozen cities at points widely scattered across the continent are completely paralyzed, and there are few signs, except perhaps in Winnipeg, where the trouble started, that it is on the wane. Fernie, Calgary, and Winnipeg are completely in a state of "internal siege;" labor men at Port William have voted favorably on the question of walking out, and property owners in Montreal are plunging heavily on insurance against damage from prospective riots.

How largely does the revolutionary element enter into the Canadian situation? Apparently very slightly. The strikers are the best organized groups of skilled workers, who have always been both the aristocrats and the conservatives of the whole labor movement. Moreover, at every point they are striking in sympathy for some specific demands on the part of one group or another. It is true that the result achieved is not dissimilar from Soviet rule, as when, in Toronto, the strike committee graciously issues an order permitting doctors, school teachers, policemen, gas and water works employees, hotel workers, etc., to continue at their posts. In Winnipeg the anti-labor newspapers were suppressed. Nowhere, as yet, however, has any statement been issued implying that the workers are trying to overthrow existing governments. When they get what they want, in the way of wages and hours, they will release the reins of authority – until next time.

Middle of Trouble

The danger is that a movement may begin in this spirit and then take the bit in its teeth and bolt beyond all control of the union leaders. No one can tell where mob psychology may carry a crowd of angry men when they are played upon by shrewd agitators of unrest, who have all to gain and nothing to lose.

Great Britain is by now safely past the crisis of her labor troubles, which not long ago threatened ruin. Speaking broadly, we in the United States have our own troubles ahead of us; and Canada is in the middle of the problem now. The Canadian worker has all the independence which the British laboring man has acquired of late years; while the Canadian employer, instead of his British brothers' frank and amicable spirit, seems to take his psychological cue from worse elements in the corresponding class in the United States. In this country, however, the employer is dealing with a group of shifting racial elements, with little homogeneity, and, until the war, one which constantly received fresh additions from immigration. Since Canadian workmen think and work so much in the spirit of their comrades in Merrie England, it would seem highly advisable that employers and public officials in Toronto, Winnipeg, and "points west" should be guided by what has been done in the British Isles. It is not too late, but if drastic action is long delayed it may be.

38 THE "SOVIET METHOD" IN WINNIPEG

The Gazette, Montreal
May 31, 1919

"It makes my blood boil to see five men, none of whom is Canadian born, or who has served overseas, run Winnipeg as they are at the present time."

This is the way one millionaire of the western metropolis, who was a pioneer there and helped build up the country, expressed his feelings today. R. J. Cromie, publisher of the Vancouver Daily Sun, who arrived in Toronto tonight, and who spent Wednesday in Winnipeg, made this statement.

"It is not a battle between employer and employee," said Mr. Cromie in discussing the Winnipeg situation, "but it is a battle between the constitutional reform and the Soviet method."

39 THIS GENERAL STRIKE IS REVOLUTION

The Winnipeg Citizen
May 31, 1919

A persistent effort is now being made by the strike leaders, through the medium of their newspaper mouthpiece, and through the medium of those who have been deceived and are not yet awake to their deception, to repudiate the fact that this is not a mere strike, but a revolution.

Senator Robertson, who is the minister of labor and a lifelong trades unionist himself, in addition to which he is the leading authority in this Dominion upon labor problems, says that it is revolution and that it is part and parcel of the "One Big Union" movement.

The "One Big Union" movement is a movement to supplant our established institutions with Soviet Government. Here is the text of a resolution that the "One Big Union" convention passed at Calgary last March:

"This convention expresses its open conviction that the system of industrial Soviet control by selection of representatives from industries is more efficient and of greater political value than the present system of government by selection from districts."

And the leaders of the present "general strike" in Winnipeg are among the chief organizers of the "One Big Union." To heap denial upon denial of any intent toward revolution will do no good. It will not change the issue nor blind the citizens of Winnipeg to the fact that Winnipeg was at first placed under an "industrial soviet," with "representatives selected from industries."

Denial after denial of intent to overturn constitutional authority will not offset the fact that constitutional authority was temporarily overturned in Winnipeg. Denial after denial of intent to revolt, will not even change the admission of the notorious "Food Committee" that "reports were rapidly coming in of children on the verge of death through want of milk."

No amount of denying will blind the fact that Winnipeg had a practical demonstration of the crass, blind brutality of the type of revolution which misrepresents the starving of innocent babies as a means to enforce "collective bargaining" which had never been challenged.

Do not be misled by the wailing of the Labor News that this is not revolution. Read these two telegrams sent by Senator Robertson, one to the mayor of Calgary and the other jointly to the mayors of Fort William and Port Arthur; they will tell you what the leading federal authority sees as the meaning of the so-called "General Strike."

This is the message sent to the mayor of Calgary:

"Winnipeg, Man., May 26, 1919.
"R. C. Marshall, Mayor of Calgary:

"Your wire. Have been here since Thursday last. Very carefully investigated the cause of the existing general strike which the strike committee claimed was called for the purpose of forcing upon certain employers the recognition of workmen's rights to collective bargaining.

"The employers affected proved conclusively that they had no objection to their employes elected as representatives of the various craft unions concerned in their industries. Have furthermore expressed perfect willingness to meet with executive officers of the various organizations if desired, but refused to deal with a body known as the Metal Trades Council, which is elected by employes in other industries outside their own.

"Twenty-four hours before the sympathetic strike was called, the Premier of Manitoba urged an adjustment of the matter in dispute by arbitration, and in a final attempt prevent the general strike, asked the committee if they would cancel it, provided the employers would agree to recognize the Metal Trades Council, to which question a negative reply was given.

"Subsequently, events have proved conclusively that the motive behind the general strike effect was for the purpose of assuming control and direction of industrial affairs; also, municipal, provincial and federal activities so far as they were being carried on in this city, and with the avowed intention of extending that control to a wider field.

"I have no hesitation in stating that the One Big Union movement is the underlying cause of the whole trouble, and that the Winnipeg general strike deserves no sympathy or support from labor organizations outside.

"(Signed) G. D. ROBERTSON,
"Minister of Labor."

Now read this other message, sent to the mayors of Fort William and Port Arthur.

Particularly note the statement that emissaries have been sent east and west to stir up the revolt in other cities. Here is the message:

"It is currently reported that a joint meeting of Fort William and Port Arthur Trades Council has been called for this afternoon for the purpose of taking sympathetic action with Winnipeg workmen now on strike.

"After carefully going into the whole situation here since last Wednesday, I am fully convinced that the general strike at Winnipeg deserves no sympathy from organized labor outside. The underlying motive in calling this strike is, in my opinion, undoubtedly intended to be a blow at international trade unions, and in support of the Big Union movement, and with the probable intention of seeking to overthrow constitutional affairs and government, both as to federal, provincial and municipal affairs.

"The justification alleged for the calling of the sympathetic strike was that certain employers refused to recognize the Metal Trades Council or right of collective bargaining to their employes. That this was an excuse and not a justification is evidenced by the fact that the Premier of Manitoba was informed by the committee the day prior to the sympathetic strike, that even though the employers would recognize or deal with the Metal Trades Council the strike would nevertheless occur.

"Emissaries sent east and west this week for purposes of obtaining sympathetic strike action in other cities is, in my opinion wholly without justification as the citizens of points outside of Winnipeg are in no way responsible for the dispute here and certainly should not be inconvenienced as result of this conflict. Would you be good enough to convey this information to the proper officers of the joint Trades and Labor Council of Fort William and Port Arthur."

40 OTTAWA'S "STUPID BLUNDER"

The Albertan, Calgary
May 31, 1919

Ottawa is handling the labor trouble like the most autocratic and impetuous and bullying slave driver of an employer. If anything were necessary to arouse labor men to action and incite the interest of the people in general, it is this announcement that the postal workers who went on strike are out of the employ of the government for all time, for ever and ever, world without end.

From the beginning the Dominion government has conducted this labor strike without any resemblance of sense. This latest move is the most stupid of all. Ottawa is responsible for the bulk of the disturbance.

41 A PROLETARIAN DICTATORSHIP

The Winnipeg Citizen,
June 3, 1919

GETTING BACK TO THE REAL ISSUE

"If an employer or a number of employers in a given industry deny to their workmen the right to bargain collectively for the sale of their services, the economic force of the workmen may properly be directed against the offender and the public will approve and sympathize. IN A GENERAL SYMPATHETIC STRIKE, THE FORCE IS DIRECTED AGAINST THE WHOLE COMMUNITY WHO ARE INNOCENT OF ANY RESPONSIBILITY FOR THE OFFENCE. PUBLIC INDIGNATION IS IMMEDIATELY AROUSED BECAUSE OF THE INCONVENIENCE, LOSS AND SUFFERING IMPOSED UPON INNOCENT PEOPLE. THEREFORE, SYMPATHETIC STRIKES MUST ALWAYS FAIL."
Hon. Gideon D. Robertson, Minister of Labor.

Such a statement as that which is quoted above, is a good thing at this time. It gets right down to fundamentals and hauls the public down to the real issue – an issue which the strike leaders are consistently attempting to becloud.

They seek, by noisy demonstrations and by repeated misrepresentations, to stampede people into forgetting what is really at stake in the struggle which is now engrossing the attention of the citizens of Winnipeg. They seek to hide the fact that their intent and aim was the establishment of "Proletarian Dictatorship," as they styled it, and they attempt to cover up the fact that Bolshevism and the "One Big Union" are behind the Winnipeg revolution.

Through their public addresses and their representations to the Provincial Legislature and the City Council, they attempt to get the public arguing about higher wages, the cost of living, and collective bargaining and what-not, and thus to trick the citizens into forgetting the injustice wrought upon innocent parties who were throttled and threatened with starvation when the strike broke out.

To a certain extent it has been necessary to correct the misrepresentations of the Sovietists and to that extent the citizens have allowed themselves to be drawn into argument and discussion of things other than the real issue – but they have never forgotten what that real issue is and, if it has been somewhat obscured while the Bolshevist propagandists' misrepresentations were being contested, the statement made by Senator Robertson once more clarifies the issue and sets it out in bold relief.

The question is not whether the Metal Trades Council started this affair with an attempt to force recognition of itself contrary to the established customs of trades union bargaining.

The moment that the sympathetic strike started, such issues became mere minor circumstances and the real issue became the principle of the general sympathetic strike itself. The general strike is Bolshevism and Bolshevism means revolution. It is a challenge to individual liberty, a challenge to decency, to honor, to justice and to our constitutional system of government.

In this general sympathetic strike, "the

force was directed against the whole community ... public indignation was immediately aroused because of the inconvenience, loss and suffering imposed upon innocent people."

Therefore, in the words of the Minister of Labor, "The Sympathetic Strike Must Fail." In Winnipeg it must be made to fail and the failure must be complete. It must be so complete as to enable Trades Unionism to shake off the parasites that infest it, in the shape of the few fanatical Bolshevists and revolutionaries who manipulated a minority vote into a tragedy for organized labor.

The defeat of the general sympathetic strike will not be a defeat for Organized Labor or Trades Unionism at all. It will be a vindication of Trades Unionism and a defeat for Bolshevism, and the men who will complete that vindication and clinch that defeat, begun by the citizens at large, will be the sane element of Labor which bears the name of Trades Unionism – an organization betrayed and tricked by the manipulation of a minority vote.

It is absolutely contrary to British fair-play, it is the very reverse of all the ideals of democracy, to victimize innocent people, to starve them, to reduce their babies to "the verge of death," to destroy or tie up their business, to forbid them transportation, and to render them subject to the dictates of a handful of fanatics who have assumed to dictate, not only to the citizens at large, but to the great body of Trades Unionists as well – who were also innocent of any intent to inflict hardship upon anybody, least of all themselves.

The more this Winnipeg situation is examined, the more monstrous appears the deception and the wilful trickery and crookedness practiced by the "One Big Union" Bolshevist fanatics upon Organized Labor and upon the public at large.

42 THE GOVERNMENT TO BLAME

The Chronicle, New Glasgow
June 3, 1919

Organs and orators presage a revolution in Canada, taking their cue from the series of strikes along the railway line from Sydney to Vancouver. Perhaps there will be a revolution and what the Winnipeg strikers are demanding is really equivalent to a revolution in labor supply. Hitherto, between Capital and Labor individual bargaining has been the rule. What the Winnipeg leaders seem to be after is "collective bargaining" which, as far as we can comprehend, means that workingmen will have a king of their own who will hire them out according to the constitution of the kingdom. Individual workers will have a vote in electing the officers after which they will do as they are told, work when they are ordered and refrain from work when ordered so to do. Whether that is the independence that comes from democratic sentiments or not, is another thing. Anyway, those are the principles of the revolution sought for in Winnipeg. We are not now going to argue against the principles of such a revolution or any; but there never was a revolution in the world that was not caused by mis-government combined with cupidity and greed. Does anyone suppose that if a man like Sir John Macdonald were now Premier and had the solid support of the Conservative party behind him that the Dominion would be troubled by these uprisings in the cities against constituted authority? Would not the face of every Conservative in Canada be set against it? The same would be true if a man like Sir Wilfrid Laurier were at the head of the Liberal party and Premier only that a lot of ill-advised Protestants would prefer a revolution than be guided by a Roman Catholic French-Canadian. The primal cause of unrest in Canada was the revolt against Quebec and Sir Wilfrid. The revolters have sown to the wind and we seem doomed to reap the whirlwind.

Protestant ministers were boasting a couple of years ago that party government in the Dominion was killed, little realizing that at the same time party political discipline was also killed. Not alone were they killing the Liberal party, the Conservative party was also being killed. A conglomeration of men were placed in power that understood they were above party as previously known and recognized, and under them the monopolists and profiteers were given the opportunity of amassing fortunes by plundering the people. The Union Government are [sic] to blame for the revolutionary tendency in the cities. In this respect the experience of Canada is in no wise different from other countries which have undergone the throes of a revolution. In everyone of them the government and the nobles were the cause. As understood in Britain and other imperial countries Canada has had no hereditary nobles, but the ambitious and unprincipled politician and the unscrupuolus [sic] and greed inspired profiteer have taken their places. The inspiration of these two classes is from the Union Government, a government which is a similitude of that of Rheoboam in Israel or the Bourbons in France. In our opinion Canada will have no peace until the Union Government is driven from power....

---

43 THE SIN AND INIQUITY OF THE STRIKE

The Gazette, Montreal
June 3, 1919

THE STRIKE SUBSIDING.

The third week of the strike in Winnipeg finds an ebbing tide. Steadily, if slowly, public services are being restored, a saner sense is causing some of the strikers to resume work, and before many days the "business as usual" sign can probably be hung out. The cost to Labor is heavy and irreparable, the loss of half a month's pay making a material gap in the year's earnings; but if the lesson is heeded the price will not be too great. Winnipeg was selected by the revolutionists for the test of strength. It contains a large foreign element easily persuaded, if not instinctively inclined, to

extreme measures, and a labor population to whom the false doctrines of socialism and the equality of men had long been preached. The conspiracy was carefully hatched, and the initial success of the sympathetic strike so considerable that the Bolsheviki leaders threw off the mask and proclaimed the rule of the Labor Committee supreme over all constituted authority. While it is now deemed prudent to sing small, the early events of the strike conclusively proved that the leaders of the movement designed to overthrow municipal, provincial and federal government, to shackle capital, to dominate industries, and to plant in Canada the vicious principles of the Russian Soviets. For a short period there was literally a disruption of the social and business life of the city, which became isolated from the outer world; but the prostration did not long endure. An aroused public spirit marshalled the great majority of the people on the side of law and order; the governments plucked up courage to assert authority; some public services were restored; the courage of the labor leaders began to ooze; and the danger point being safely passed, a gradual amelioration has set in.

The strike, conceived in sin and born in iniquity, could have no other ending. There are some dangerous, reckless socialists in Canada, but they are a mere fraction of the people, and this Dominion does not give fertile soil for the propagation of their teaching. Nor could a more unpropitious time have been chosen to overthrow law, order and constituted government. There is unemployment, and the cost of living is unprecedentedly high; but no great degree of intelligence is required in workingmen to know that unemployment cannot be relieved by closing down industries, and that the cost of living cannot be reduced by increasing the price of production by higher wages, or shorter hours, or both. The unrest does, indeed, continue. Strikes have been ordered in other cities in support and sympathy with Winnipeg strikes which have more or less disturbed the communities in which they occur. It is possible the epidemic has not yet run its full course, but the fever is less virulent. The collapse of the Winnipeg movement will have a repressing influence elsewhere, and the warning sounded from that city will not go unheeded.

---

44 VETERANS DEMAND ACTION

The Star, Toronto
June 4, 1919

NO MINCING OF WORDS WHEN VETS SEE NORRIS

– Winnipeg is still deadlocked, more strikers are returning to work, but returned soldiers among the strikers are very aggressive and are keeping alive the hope of the labor forces. Three thousand veterans and many others marched to the Parliament Buildings at noon Monday and insisted that the Government pass a compulsory collective bargaining Act, submit the matter to a referendum or resign. Premier Norris refused. Statements that a vast majority of the Province was against the Government evoked tremendous cheers.

A. E. "Jack" Moore did not appear at the head of the delegation. This time his place was taken by Comrade Bray, who asked the Premier whether he knew anything about the reports that the Fort Garry Horse had been ordered to "stand to" during the parade, and that machine guns were concealed about the Parliament Buildings. The Premier denied any knowledge, and again was cheered.

Comrade Bray said there was a plot to put bombs on the persons of the strike leaders and arrest them.

Backed Up By Colleagues.

Premier Norris when receiving the delegation had the Provincial Treasurer on his left, the Attorney-General on his right, and the Minister of Education in the rear. Great care was taken to only allow veterans enter the building. Norris intimated he was opposed to making sympathetic strikes criminal.

Comrade Bray said: "Boys, you have signified confidence in your committee and

its ability to handle the case. Please don't interrupt the speakers. If anyone tells lies there are enough of us here who know the facts to confound them without you butting in."

"Now Mr. Premier, on behalf of the returned soldiers of the Province, I have the honor to present you with a copy of resolution passed by our Executive Committee and the men present. It says 'Sir, whereas we learn through Senator Robertson and Sir Robert Borden that the Dominion Government have no authority to legislate collective bargaining, and whereas the same authorities say the matter is within the jurisdiction of the Provincial bodies only, therefore be it resolved that we, the returned soldiers of this Province, herewith demand that such legislation be passed by the legislature of this Province and thus remove a cause of unrest. Also we demand immediate withdrawal of the ultimatum to Provincial employes and their reinstatement without discrimination. In the event of your not being ready to comply with these demands, we call upon your Government to resign." (Tremendous applause.)

Says Norris Is Afraid.

Continuing Bray said: "We want an answer, Mr. Premier, to the demands we made on Friday and Saturday when your reply was anything but satisfactory, and left the impression that you were afraid or incapable of dealing satisfactorily with the situation. After another 48-hours' consideration we would like to get your answer, re legislation and other questions. That is all for the present." (Applause.)

Premier Norris replied: "Mr. Bray and gentlemen, you have brought an important question before me, on Friday and Saturday and again today in the shape of an ultimatum, backed up by an immense throng of peaceful citizens and in a gentlemanly way. I thank you for the quiet way in which you have presented your case. You have said that you are defenders of constitutional Government and methods, and I believe you are. We are a constitutional Government, elected by a large majority, to conduct the affairs of the Province to the best of our ability.

How far we have succeeded is for the people to say. We have done our best to act along constitutional lines and have stuck to that, and intend to. You believe that this Government should take some drastic measures to back up the principle you are behind. As I have said, we represent the people of all the Provinces, [*sic*] until the minds of the people have changed. There is a constitutional means of getting rid of a Government if you so desire.

Don't Represent Whole People.

"I have made certain representations to the newspapers and the City Council. You asked us on Saturday that we convene the Legislature for a purpose. There is a method to be followed. However much respect we may have for speeches you have made and for the large audience gathered to second them, we represent the whole people and their representatives have to be consulted and constitutional methods followed. If you represented all people, we could decide right here whether the Government should step down or not.

"I agree with you in many things, on others I do not. I have no authority to say to you that I will call a special session and pass legislation. You say we have jurisdiction. I cannot say whether we have or not. I want to say now that the constitutional way to get rid of this Government remains and the people must be consulted. We have to hear from them and for the Government or a representative of the Government to make a decision would be entirely unconstitutional, much as I might like to please this gathering.

Opposed to Sympathetic Strike.

"I am in sympathy personally with collective bargaining but wholly opposed to sympathetic strikes. Sympathetic strikes on public utilities are wholly wrong. The railwaymen right now are mediating, and if given support they should work out the solution. Collective bargaining does not depend upon legislation, but on agreements between employers and employes. The legislation might be disregarded by somebody. The running trades have a collective agreement and if we are not panicky but give

dispassionate support to them, I am confident they will secure a settlement, not only to help organized labor, but put it on a footing it never has been on before. It is advisable that settlement along those lines be tried with the sympathy of the public. I am opposed to trying to force anybody by law lest, injustice be caused. My colleagues have the same ideas. Wherever economic force is allied against an innocent community it never succeeded. No sympathetic strike is wanted unless there is a desperate injustice. You think there is injustice and have put a very large proportion of the community to inconvenience, which is wrong."

Won't Be Effective.

"But to say sympathetic strikes are unlawful will not be effective if placed on the statute books because if a large number of sensible men think it unjust, it would have to be removed. The great majority of people of the Province outside the city are not aware of the issue and have to be considered. Just as soon as the people say I should retire I will step down cheerfully. I appreciate the confidence thus far given the Government. We have been passing through troublesome times and a reaction was bound to come.

"Canadian and British people do provide religious and political liberty. We want that to continue and to continue peacefully and surely here in this part of the Empire that is the mother of free Parliaments."

Voice: "Give us your answer."

Premier Norris: "I have given you the answer. I have no constitutional authority to say that it will be done. I cannot make pledges I have no right to make. I am willing to do everything possible to secure settlement. I appreciate that you think differently and that you have a large gathering to back you up." (Applause.)

Comrade Bray: "We are disappointed because we impressed on you that we demanded action. We have not exceeded constitutional lines. We are not a mere handful, but represent all the men who have been away and come back to the Province. (Applause). You say we represent but one part of the community, but I say on their behalf that we have backing and support, morally and materially, of an overwhelming majority of citizens of Manitoba, and what we want to know is, if you have, after 72 hours consideration, changed your attitude as to collective bargaining. According to that rag, The Telegram, you promised the City Council to give the matter your serious consideration. Senator Robertson, Senator and Strike-breaker, man who comes from the home of the dead, speaking as an official, says the matter is not within the jurisdiction of the Federal, but of Provincial power. Premier Borden said likewise. If the Premier of the Dominion and Minister of Labor don't know what they are talking about, then to whom shall we appeal? In 1914 and 1915 we came to your support, and thousands of us voted for you as a strong-minded and straight-forward man. Those we represent are men. Those supporting the Committee of One Thousand are not men. That committee represents the same bunch of boodlers who plundered this Province to the verge of bankruptcy. (Applause).

Calls It "Dirty Sheet."

"Reading this dirty sheet, and this dirty sheet, and this dirty sheet, (exhibiting three full page ads of the Citizens' Committee) the Government says it can do nothing until the sympathetic strike is called off. I tell you on behalf of all, we will never call off the sympathetic strike. (Terrific cheering.) You speak of innocent who suffered in the strike, But [sic] the Committee of One Thousand is supported by Senator Joe Flavelle (loud booing inside, taken up by thousands outside,) and we are told there are twenty new millionaires in Toronto since the war."

Side With Boodlers.

A voice: "Three hundred and forty-nine in Canada."

Comrade Bray: "They have purchased real estate to the extent of thousands of dollars and have made money out of the innocent, while we were over there defending the land we love. This Citizens' Committee are men who have raised the rents on the boys since we have come home. Mr. Premier you, by your silence, side with this bunch of boodlers and shameless profiteers.

If you are so much on the side of labor, why do you not dare to come over to some of our meetings and say so? You say that to resign would be violation of constitutional authority. If I remember rightly one plank in your platform was the referendum and recall. If you still believe in that, put it into operation and let the people you misrepresent decide. We contend that if you have nothing more to tell us, it is proof of your incompetency to handle a situation like this.

Will Never Surrender.

"We on the floor of the House and a great delegation outside represent 150,000 citizens of Winnipeg, who number 200,000. (Great cheering.) As to the running trades, those old tories of the labor movement are butting in on something that does not concern them, but rather than impede a settlement, we have no objection. We have tried to leave you and the Citizens' Committee a pillow to fall on, and the railway men are still mediating, but on the great question at issue, we will stand for no mediation and no compromise. Until the rivers run dry, organized labor will not compromise on that principle."

Hears of Bomb Plot.

"Superintendent Williams has notified six phone operators and the Committee of One Thousand that the Soviet at the Industrial Bureau will not allow the Telephone Commission to take back the girls. I have reliable and authentic information with names to show there is a plot in this city to place upon the persons of leading strikers bombs, so that the men can be arrested on a charge of carrying explosives. That is the plan of our opponents. Among other things, since the interview on Saturday I am told the military authorities have posted concealed machine guns in and around this building. I would like to know if you can contradict it. We will take your word for it.

"Mayor Gray has said the Government has no reason to hesitate about passing an order-in-Council, that it has passed one in thirty-five or forty minutes. I would like, rather, we insist, that you put into operation a referendum, and we, ourselves, are quite prepared to abide by the verdict of the constitutional majority." (Cheers.)

Comrade Bray then called for a fair hearing for Comrade Bathie. Immediately veterans shouted "No, fifty-fifty." Premier Norris, however, interrupted to say emphatically, "As to the troops standing to and machine-guns posted, that is my first intimation, and I know nothing about it." (Loud applause.)

Suggests a Compromise.

Comrade Bathie: "The man who is not behind the labor movement in [sic] not a man. In all squareness to the community let's go over to the Industrial Bureau, with returned men only and get down to some concrete basis as to what returned soldiers really want. Put your cards on the table and mediate in a gentlemanly discussion. It's only the returned movement that concerns me. What happened on Saturday? An element was creeping in which tended to be detrimental only not [sic] to the returned movement but to labor."

A hurricane of "No's" greeted this statement. Also, "Sit down." "shut up."

Comrade Parnell: "In reply to Comrade Bathie, I would say the suggestion about the Industrial Bureau comes too late. As to the element that got into the parade on Saturday, a few wise heads got together to-day and took steps to keep out the other element.

"The Premier by not passing compulsory legislation is hurting the greatest part of the community, if he passed it, he would only hurt one thousand. (Laughter.) I think the Premier would like to please us but one thing is stopping him. So long as the Premier allows that bunch of thieves and rogues to control his hands are tied."

Comrade Bray: "Mr. Premier, I must inform you that to-morrow morning we shall be back again and will want an emphatic statement as to where you and your Government stand, whether you are prepared to call a special session and if not, when you will give people a chance to give their verdict and confirm your actions or vote you out."

The meeting then closed with the singing of the "National Anthem" and "God Save Our Splendid Men."

A Great War Veterans Association demonstration held at the rear of City Hall. Mayor Gray is standing under the "Down with Bolshevism" sign, June 4, 1919.

[Published by permission of the Provincial Archives of Manitoba]

45 CHURCH AND LABOR

The Albertan, Calgary
June 4, 1919

The Methodist conference ran true to form yesterday morning – if such a race track expression is permissible in referring to the church – when the Alberta conference decided to wire a protest to the Canadian government protesting against the dismissal of the postal workers on strike. The church takes the right view point. The government has decided to blacklist its own employes because they took decided action on an important occasion.

A prominent Calgary minister, Rev. A. McTaggart, in a very excellent sermon on Sunday night defended the sympathetic strike. There are two very important expressions from two different sources.

It is very much to the credit of the church that it is considering these very important questions. It is possible that Mr. Parsons of the Canadian Manufacturers' association, and Sir Joseph Flavelle may disapprove of the action of the conference. The church has too long been dominated and influenced by such people. But now the church is becoming what it always should have been, the big heart and spirit of the entire people.

The church is taking its proper place in the life of the people when it undertakes from its high and noble position in life, to help to solve the great problems which confront the people.

---

46 POLITICIANS AND THE STRIKE

The Post, Sydney, N.S.
June 4, 1919

AN INSTRUCTIVE SYMPOSIUM.

On a motion for adjournment by Dr. Blake, member for Winnipeg North, in the House of Commons, the Winnipeg strike situation became the subject of a parliamentary debate on Monday. Dr. Blake's avowed purpose in bringing the matter up was to precipitate a discussion, which might contain constructive suggestions, and thus help towards a settlement of the distressing situation at Winnipeg. The chief participants in the symposium thus opened were Dr. Blake himself- [sic] Ernest Lapointe of Kamouraska, Quebec, Major Andrews of Centre Winnipeg, W. A. Buchanan of Medicine Hat, Hon. Arthur Meighen, D. D. MacKenzie, and Sir Robert Borden.

If the discussion contained no very deinite [sic] suggestions as to a way out of the Winnipeg deadlock, it gave at least pretty accurate views of the political stature of those participating in it.

Dr. Blake was non-committal, as became one hailing from the storm-centre. Major Andrews, who also represents a Winnipeg constituency, and one which is a great labor centre, showed himself moderately sympathetic with the strikers. Mr. Lapointe's contribution to the fund of wisdom on how to settle Labor disputes, was a partisan attack on the Government, coupled with a vicious jab or two at Sir Joseph Flavelle. Mr. D. D. MacKenzie first attacked the Government, – as was eminently fitting in a parliamentary official receiving $7,000 per session from the Government for that sort of thing, – and then made what was probably the most fantastic proposal which has been seriously put forward in parliament for many a long day. This was nothing less than that a sort of Labor Sumpreme Court be established for all the provinces, with authority to review industrial disputes, and forbid strikes!

Mr. Buchanan, who comes from a prairie constituency, thought the solution of the trouble was to be found in the application of that Western panacea for economic ills, free trade, or at least a reduction of customs taxation.

It is pretty obvious that no administration could get much that is helpful from such short-visioned surveys of a national problem. Not one of the speakers, except Hon. Arthur Meighen and the Prime Minister, was a parrently [sic] capable of discussing the matter, without an eye to party strategy, or to the votes in his constituency. It is just such speeches that are most to blame for much of the Labor unrest, as well as for most of the sectional and racial prejudices in the country.

Mr. Meighen reported to the House what he had seen and learned at Winnipeg. He described the Winnipeg upheaval as a tentative revolution rather than a strike. He declared that the citizens of Winnipeg were as adamant in their determination to defeat the movement, and made it clear that the Government would co-operate with the people in this endeavor.

Sir Robert Borden outlined the Government's policy for dealing with the Canadian Labor situation, which he described as showing less serious features than that in Europe, or even in the United States. He indicated that legislation would shortly be submitted, to faciltate [sic] the settlement of industrial disputes, by enabling employers and employees to get together more readily for the consideration of mutual view-points. Such questions as working hours and collective bargaining, he pointed out, come under the jurisdiction, not of the Dominion Parliament, but of the several Local Legislatures.

Despite some of the partisan and narrow-visioned views it elicited, the debate should do some good, for it proved beyond question that the revolutionaries of Winnipeg will receive no consideration whatever from the Government, and that organized labor, standing up in its own strength and advocating its legitimate demands, can accomplish infinitely more than by linking itself up with alien and lawless forces. The statements of the Prime Minister and of Hon. Arthur Meighen will be reassuring alike to Labor interests, and to the citizenship of Canada.

---

47 THE LESSONS OF SEATTLE

The Post, Regina
June 5, 1919

The Seattle Strike

The Western Labor News, official bulletin of the strike committee in Winnipeg, contains a sentence that is of greatest significance. In dealing with the question of food distribution, it remarks, "Bearing in mind the lesson we had learned from the Seattle strike a short time ago, the Central Strike Committee struck off a special Food Committee to deal with the question."

"Bearing in mind the lesson we had learned from the Seattle strike," is a phrase of much significance. It identifies the controlling minds of the Winnipeg strike quite definitely with the controlling minds of the Seattle strike. That seems to us a fair inference, and it is important in this connection to remember the significance of the Seattle strike.

The Seattle strike is regarded everywhere in the United States as the first and probably the last outbreak of Bolshevism in that country. It is regarded as the first, because the symptoms were unmistakable. The strike committee, in its first bulletins, made it clear that the overthrow of the government was aimed at.

Mayor Ole Hanson is acclaimed throughout the United States as the man who put down the Bolshevik uprising in Seattle. Anarchists in the United States do him similar honor, for he has been deluged with threatening letters and has had more than one bomb addressed to him. Yet the fact seems to be simply that Mayor Hanson adopted only the reasonable attitude, declaring that authority in the city of Seattle was vested in the city hall and would be kept there.

What broke the Seattle strike was the attitude of the real labor union men, as distinguished from the Socialists and Anarchists, who had foisted themselves upon the union movement. They went on strike willingly enough when their leaders called it, but when, a few days later, it dawned on them that their strike was regarded not as a labor demonstration, but as a Bolshevik uprising, and further that there was good ground for such a view, the strike simply collapsed. The labor men went back to work regardless of the orders of the strike committee. The number of men on strike, at the time the strike committee finally succumbed, was a bare handful.

It was the workers, the trades unionists, who broke the strike at Seattle.

---

48 STRIKES AND WAGES

The Gazette, Montreal
June 9, 1919

As a consequence of the recent happenings in Winnipeg and Toronto, the One Big Union idea seems to have received a very necessary setback, necessary in the interests of the community at large, and not less necessary to the legitimate progress of the organized labor movement. Had the Winnipeg attempt succeeded, the consequences to Canadian industry would have been serious and far-reaching. Capital, without which no industry can be carried on, would have been frightened out of the country, and no new capital from outside sources would have been forthcoming for industrial purposes. Production would have declined and the opportunities for employment would have decreased. The process would have been rapid or gradual, according to the spread of the poison, but it would unquestionably have occurred.

If the facts of the Winnipeg strike are studied, it will be seen that the principle of collective bargaining was never the issue. It was the watchword, or rather the catchword of the strikers, but only as a cloak for the real movement. The employers in the trades originally affected did not deny the right of collective bargaining on the part of the crafts concerned. They were willing to bargain, but the employees were not. The general strike was resorted to, not for the purpose of collective bargaining, but for the purpose of exacting from the employers the maximum of the demands made. From the moment the general strike was ordered, there was no question of bargaining, collective or otherwise. It was a show of force, meant to be just that. The position of the strike leaders was this: "We are not prepared to bargain with you. We intend to compel you to grant all the demands made by these trades. Your continued refusal will be the ruin of your industries." To the general public, the attitude of the strikers was this: "We do not care anything about your comfort, your interests or your rights. We are going to make it so unpleasant for you that you will be forced to side with us, and the longer you wait the more it is going to cost you." Had this attempt succeeded, in regard to the trades first involved, it would have succeeded equally well with other trades and would, in time, have gone the round of all. That was what the citizens of Winnipeg saw before them. They understood the situation and, to their credit, accepted the challenge. Other cities in Canada owe them a debt for their courage and their determination.

A correspondent has drawn attention to the fact that the United States has escaped troubles of this kind, and he wonders whether this is due to the fact that the labor leader in the United States is more capable, or to the fact that the employer in the United States is more diplomatic than the employer in this country. He suggests that the employer in the United States is ready to deal more generously with his employees because he knows that what does not go to the employees will largely go to the Government in taxes. Canada is not less likely to enjoy immunity from business taxation for a period of years than is the United States, and the method suggested of meeting the demands of labor is as applicable here as there. It would, for a time, and to a degree, solve the problem for the employer, but certain possible objections suggest themselves. To begin with, the wage standard would be increased substantially, without regard to the actual value of the service rendered, which, as an economic proposition, is undesirable. Not all industries are equally prosperous, though they be engaged in similar lines of production, and the wage standard which might be borne successfully by one industry would be ruinous in another. And even if all were able to support such a standard, the result would be to increase still more the costs of production, costs which are bearing more and more heavily now upon the consumer, and, particularly, the consumer whose income is fixed. There is also the effect which such an expedient would have upon the process of taxation. If the profits of industry are reduced through wage increases, the State is deprived proportionately of its estimated revenue. The consequence would necessarily be a new distribution of the tax, because the State must have the money. If the State found itself unable to collect this tax at one point, it would collect it at another. In the case suggested, the money would be in the hands of the worker, and the tax would have to be so revised as to reach the worker's income. The safer plan would seem to be to pay to the worker a fair price for his work, to base that price upon economic laws, having regard to fair market values of the products of labor. A wage increase which carried with it a liability to further taxation would confer no real benefit. The recipient would be no better off and would soon make the discovery.

---

49 TRADE UNIONS AND THE BIG UNION

The Star, Toronto
June 9, 1919

The workman who believes in organized trades unionism as we have had it in Canada and the workman who believes in the One Big Union idea have a pretty strong difference of opinion separating them.

Those who support the idea of One Big Union are evidently men who have grown impatient with the progress made by organized labor under the system of craft unions, and propose to take a swift short cut to the results they desire.

In this country we have international labor organizations, with the result that the members of a craft union in Toronto are connected up with similar workers all over Canada and the United States, and in the event of a local strike the union here has the financial backing of an organization that covers the continent.

The advocate of the One Big Union idea does not care anything about such backing, and says he doesn't need it. His plan is to include all Canadian labor in one group, declare a general strike, produce a paralysis of all industry and business, dictate terms, and force their acceptance within a week. His contention is that large funds are not needed, because a general strike would produce results quickly. His plan is to stop

everything and demand what he wants. It looks simple and direct. At times he speaks of it as a dictatorship of the protletariat [*sic*]. It is very different from industrial unionism, and it aims at mastery quite outside the field of labor.

There are 260,000 labor unionists in Canada. In a population of 7,500,000 it is estimated that one-third, or 2,500,000, are wage-earners, so that 260,000 unionists would be but one-tenth of the total number of wage-earners in Canada. As compared with that the local carpenters, in their affiliation with the Amalgamated Carpenters, belong to an international organization with a membership of 264,000. The advocate of One Big Union for Canada rests his whole case on the general strike as a means of holding up everything and dictating terms. His reliance is on force, compulsion. The regular trades union idea is to rely upon the progress that can be made by organization and education.

As for the opponents of trade unionism who insist on keeping open shops or who insist that they will negotiate with nobody but their own employes they are considered to be short-sighted by moderate labor leaders. The advocates of craft unionism declare that there is a natural development taking place, and the resistance which some employers give it is playing into the hands of the One Big Union people. The craft unionist believes that a natural development of unionism is as desirable as it is inevitable. On the railways, for instance, the engineers, conductors, brakemen, etc., do collective bargaining with the company. On a railway, or in almost any shop industry, if one union were to go on strike all the others would be affected, and, if the strike lasted long, all would be idle. If they unite and bargain collectively an agreement is reached with them all at one time and covering a set period. Instead of craft unionism the natural development is towards industrial unionism.

The strikes in the metal trades in Winnipeg and Toronto were owing to the refusal of the employers to negotiate with metal trades councils of the workers. In England the employers would, as a matter of course, have negotiated with such councils, and not only with such a local council for a city, but with a national council representing workers in metal. In England where the men have not such general organization the Government requires it of them, sets it up for them in order to ensure adequate machinery for authoritative negotiation. The Whitely plan is based on this principle. In the United States and with some firms in Canada, where the Rockefeller plan of conference between employers and workers has been introduced, the express provision is that all the workers shall have their common interests represented in conferences and negotiations. The idea is that instead of a single craft acting for itself all the crafts, all the workers in an industry, shall negotiate collectively with the employing company. Out of this plan, it is claimed, comes something like dependable agreements and stable conditions and a sense of community of interest among all concerned.

50 LIBERAL FENCE-SITTERS

The Times, Toronto
June 9, 1919

THE THREE C. B.'s.

Mr. Ernest Lapointe has announced in Parliament that he favors collective bargaining. What variety of collective bargaining does he mean? There are three sorts. First, there is the open discussion of all the workers in a certain specified industry with the employers in that industry, by means of a get-together committee equally representing both sides. That is commendable.

The second sort is based on the federation of all unions in any way related to a group of industries dealing with similar products. A good example is found in the Metal Trades. All metal-working Unions have a central council which undertakes to deal directly with employers who have disputes with their men. But it is more than probable that this council may represent some Unions which have no direct relation with the plants affected by the unrest.

For instance, the sheet-metal manufac-turers have no moulders, blacksmiths or shiprivetters in their employment, but the Metal Trades Council is representative of these Union men as well as of the sheet-metal workers. There are plenty of employers, desirous of treating their own men fairly, who see in the interference of such a central council a most objectionable situation. They are willing to bargain with the Unions whose members they employ, but unwilling to accept the dictation of outsiders. In other words they favor collective bargaining No. 1, but oppose collective bargaining No. 2.

The third sort of "C. B." is that essayed in Winnipeg and Toronto. All the Unions elect a central committee with power to call out workers of all kinds, unless employers having difficulty with their men accept the rulings of this central organization. Such a Committee takes no cognizance of agreements made by any Union with the employers. It seeks to dictate to all employers at the expense of the community. That is frank Bolshevism, the One Big Union favored by the I. W. W.'s, the Reds and all the offensive elements in the population. Collective Bargaining No. 3 aims at a subversion of constituted authority. It is an attempt to produce revolution.

Mr. Lapointe should have said which form of collective bargaining he approved. Only the politician of uncommon slimness welcomes the opportunity of saying something that can be construed in three different ways.

51 EMPLOYERS IN THE WRONG

The Sun, Vancouver
June 10, 1919

To all reasonable men it must be evident that, with regard to the question of collective bargaining, the position taken by Winnipeg employers is untenable. If there is revolutionary threat on one side, there is intolerable arrogance on the other.

The Winnipeg employers declare they "will settle all disputes with unions of their own employees." This means that the employer will consent to receive a committee of his men when he is not busy at something else, and will be decently civil to them unless he happens to be in bad humor. At bottom, however, the terms of employment will be such as he chooses to offer. The men's part in the negotiations will be to express their thanks.

As a concession, the Winnipeg employers will "fall back on the Industrial Disputes Act" when differences arise. The Industrial Disputes Act provides, in substance, that there shall be an enquiry and a recommendation by an appointed board, before there is a strike. As the recommendation, when made, is not binding on either side, the employers would still be in a position to do as they like.

Industrial peace cannot be secured on this basis. When the Winnipeg employers try to pass this proposition off as "collective bargaining," they are indulging in what some men call misrepresentation and others describe as plain lying. Organized labor can not surrender on this point without being destroyed.

---

52 THE FOURTH WEEK

The Globe, Toronto
June 10, 1919

THE SYMPATHETIC STRIKE.

Winnipeg entered the fourth week of the great industrial struggle that has seriously crippled the city's business with the determination to make an end of the sympathetic strike – involving public services – as a factor in disputes between Capital and Labor. The issue is clearly recognized as of supreme inportance. The original cause of the upheaval – a strike for the eight-hour day on the part of the metal workers of the city and for the recognition by the three employing firms concerned of the right of collective bargaining through the agency of the Metal Trades Council acting for the employees – has receded into the background.

The bulk of the citizens of Winnipeg were undoubtedly in sympathy with the demand of the metal workers that their Council should be acknowledged in negotiations concerning wages and hours of work. But when the Labor leaders of Winnipeg endeavored to bring pressure to bear on the metal manufacturers by a general strike the citizens began to see what the "One Big Union" idea would involve were it to replace the system of trade union organization.

By means of the general sympathetic strike the people of Winnipeg – who were not parties to the dispute between the metal manufacturers and their employees – have been deprived of deliveries of milk, bread, and other necessaries of life. Postal and telegraphic communication has been cut off. The publication of newspapers was for a time prevented. Members of the fire brigade deserted their posts, and the protection of the city against fire had to be undertaken by volunteers. The street railway service was put out of commission, and after three weeks has not been resumed. Sanitary workers in the city's employ left garbage uncollected and streets uncleaned, to the danger of the public health.

These intolerable conditions have aroused the people of Winnipeg to the menace of the sympathetic strike. Behind all the other perils and difficulties loomed the fear that the police force was not loyal to the citizens, and could not be depended upon to protect them in case of disturbance of the peace. This fear was not groundless, for it was known that the police of Winnipeg were prepared to go out on strike when the call to do so was issued by the strike leaders. Faced by the grim fact that the general sympathetic strike in its results meant Soviet rule, the citizens of Winnipeg organized to carry on the public services of the city and their own business affairs without the help of the strikers. To a considerable degree they have succeeded. The city begins to get back to normal, and day by day more of the strikers give up the fight. The leaders of the "One Big Union" do not admit this to be the case, but it is significant that their efforts are now directed to the extension of the general strike to the steam railways of the Dominion. They hope that by putting the railways out of business the urban population will be starved into submission through the failure of the food supply.

A recent issue of The Labor News, contrary to what the people of Toronto know to be the truth, declares that "every hour the strike is spreading," and that "not one city that has struck in sympathy with us has gone back." It may be that technically the Toronto union men who went on strike did so in sympathy with the Toronto metal workers and not with those of Winnipeg, but the fact remains that a sympathetic strike, engineered in this city by supporters of the "One Big Union," failed utterly to produce the anticipated result and was promptly ended.

---

53 DEMANDS OF THE CITIZENS' COMMITTEE OF 1000

The Manitoba Free Press, Winnipeg
June 4, 1919

TO THE CITIZENS OF WINNIPEG

Owing to the deep interest of all Citizens in the labors of the "Citizens' Committee of One Thousand" which you organized to cope with the situation brought on by the present strike, we the Executive, desire to report:

Following your instructions to maintain Law and Order, and assist the Civic Authorities in operating the Public Utilities, several thousand citizens have laid aside their regular work, closed up their places of business and devoted themselves day and night to the work left by those called out by the strike Committee.

This large body of loyal, self-sacrificing Citizens has made it possible for this community for the past twenty days to have Water, Fire Protection, Bread, Milk, etc., which has involved the constant feeding and transporting of large numbers of workers.

Citizens have further assisted in re-establishing Telephone service at the request of the Manitoba Government, and at the instance of the Federal authorities, have helped in the distribution of vast quantities of mail and in re-establishing Postal Service.

There has also been organized during the period the Public Press was muzzled the "Winnipeg Citizen," a daily paper, that the Community might have the facts of the strike faithfully presented.

Owing to the persistent efforts of certain individuals to misrepresent and disturb the good work and intentions of these Citizens, it is only fair to again state that the "Citizens' Committee of One Thousand" has, at no time, taken either the side of the Employer or Employee, but has, at all times, devoted itself faithfully to the grave matters which involved the Community at large.

The Committee's stand that matters affecting the rights of the whole Community must first be dealt with before private disputes, such as that of the Metal Trades, could be taken up, has been endorsed as sound and just by the Dominion Government, Provincial Government and Civic Authorities.

Premier Norris, within the last few days, has reaffirmed – notwithstanding intimidation and threat – that the wrong done must first be righted and this "Sympathetic Strike" called off before minor issues can be considered. When our Constituted Authorities, as represented by the Dominion and Provincial Governments and City Council, had answered the challenge to Law and Order, thrown down by the Strike Committee, and had thereby endorsed the Committee's position, the Committee immediately lent every assistance towards bringing about negotiations which they sincerely hope will eventually lead to a settlement of the Metal Trades dispute.

The Undesirable Citizens In Our Midst

How much longer is the alien to run amuck, to insult our flag, take it by force from Canadian-born citizens in our streets, continue his threatening attitude to Law and Order, is the question thousands are daily demanding our Citizens' Committee of One Thousand to answer.

During the past four years when aged fathers and mothers, when wives and sisters were bullied and insulted by this element, they consoled each other by saying: "Just wait till the boys come home."

Must Deal With The Alien Now

There are some 27,000 registered alien enemies in Winnipeg district. The same "Reds" who are prominent leaders in this strike, led them during the war to hamper and block in every conceivable way, recruiting our reinforcements and supplies from going forward to the front.

The demand pouring in on our Citizens' Committee from thousands of loyal citizens that the alien question has reached the limit of endurance and must be dealt with now is receiving your Committee's grave consideration.

Citizens' Committee of One Thousand.

---

54 SOLDIERS FIRST FOR VACANT JOBS

The Manitoba Free Press, Winnipeg
June 5, 1919

The prime duty before this community is to place the returned soldiers in good positions in which they can earn a suitable living.

There has been great difficulty in doing this heretofore because in thousands of cases aliens had pre-empted the soldiers' jobs while the boys were on duty at the front.

These aliens held on to their jobs and were backed in this determination by the REDS – all of them Stay-at-Homes who had been bitter in their opposition to the war.

The Calgary convention formally by resolution identified itself with the aliens and pledged them its support and protection in the positions which they had captured at home while our boys were capturing German positions overseas.

From these positions, these aliens, with the assistance of their friends of the Calgary convention – Russell, Johns, Armstrong, Scoble and others – have now fired themselves.

Public opinion should see to it that they stay fired until every returned soldier is provided with work.

SOLDIERS FIRST must be the slogan of employers and of the public.

The alien has had four years of safe work at high wages while Canadian boys were fighting in France and Flanders.

The soldiers are now home; the vacant jobs are theirs by right; and they must get them.

Choose between the
Soldiers who protected you
and the
Aliens who threaten you!

Citizens' Committee of One Thousand.

---

55 SOLDIERS AND DEMOCRACY

The Star, Montreal,
June 7, 1919

The Winnipeg War Veterans are definitely abandoning their neutrality on the strike and lining up against the agitators. They are true to their colors. As one of them puts it, "Our 'One Big Union' is the Union Jack." Having fought for democracy overseas they could not fight against it here.

Naturally the most of them being workmen themselves, are in sympathy with the legitimate demands of labor. At the outset of this strike they quite naturally supported the demands of the strikers. But when the demand began to grow from the legitimate industrial sphere into the political range, and when it became unmistakably obvious that the moving spirits directing the unrest were men determined to overthrow the existing democratic institutions, if they could; men to whom democracy is a byword; men of no country and of no flag;; [sic] men swollen with undigested socialism and pledged to the Red Flag, the eyes of the soldiers just as naturally were opened and they took their stand in Winnipeg as in Flanders Field for the plain and simple realities upon which British democracy is based and is building – for a government, of the people and by the people, rather than of a class, for any class.

There is no question but that in their stand in this matter the Veterans reflect the great body of Canadian public opinion. These Red Flaggers mean no more in the current of our political life than the scum on the surface of Montreal harbor signifies in comparison with the great current of the St. Lawrence moving steadily on its appointed way.

56 WINNIPEG WAR VETERANS ACT

The Leader, Regina
June 7, 1919

Significant developments in connection with the general sympathetic strike in Winnipeg have taken place within the last few days, according to reports in the daily press of that city, and, inasmuch as other Western papers are still deprived of a telegraphic service out of Winnipeg, The Leader, in common with other papers, must await the arrival of Winnipeg papers in order to learn what is taking place in the metropolis.

On Wednesday, the Central Strike Committee issued a new order for the complete tie-up of Winnipeg by calling out all union men who were at work, with the exception of the police. As a result there was a cessation of milk and bread deliveries on Thursday morning, and the city authorities were compelled to take over the distribution of these necessities of life and to provide protection to all bread and milk plants and for the delivery of their products. Distribution is being carried on through all the schools in the city. Most theatres, including moving picture, vaudeville and legitimate, were closed, although hitherto they have been allowed to remain open. Many of the cafes, restaurants and lunch counters were forced to close and the down-town food situation made more serious. At the Labor Hall it was stated that every eating house in the city would be forced to close its doors sooner or later. Even the grave diggers were called upon to quit work.

An even more significant development, following the demonstrations in favor of the strikers at the Parliament Buildings and City Hall by large bodies of men who professed to be returned soldiers and to speak for the Great War Veterans' Association, was the action of the executive of the Winnipeg branch of the G. W. V. A. in utterly repudiating these demonstrations, and the meetings held and resolutions passed in the name of returned soldiers.

The G. W. V. A. executive went further and officially placed itself on record as being no longer neutral and as unqualifiedly ready to support the Dominion, Provincial and civic authorities in the full exercise of their constitutional duties, and as being prepared to suppress all alien and other agitators, Bolshevism, and any attempt to introduce soviet principles in Canada and the British Empire. A great demonstration of loyal returned soldiers followed, in which 5,000 returned men participated and formally conveyed assurance of their unqualified support to Premier Norris and Mayor Gray.

The Veterans are now alive to the fact that the Strike Committee has been endeavoring to use the returned soldiers and sow dissension in their ranks, and the declaration by a man named Bray who usurped the right to speak for the returned men, that he was a Sovietist and in favor of a soviet form of government in Canada, and that they intended to upset the constitution of the Great War Veterans' Association, was the last straw, which, coupled with the final act of the Strike Committee in endeavoring to starve Winnipeg into submission, has led thousands of returned soldiers to appreciate the fact that it is not a strike for recognition of unions, collective bargaining or a living wage that is in progress, but an out and out political revolution which seeks to destroy all existing forms of government, national institutions and organizations, including even such bodies as the Great War Veterans' Association.

It has also become more and more evident that this so-called strike is an attempt on the part of Reds to get control of industry in order to keep all non-English speaking and aliens permanently in their present positions, which they captured during the war, and made good wages, while the soldiers were capturing German positions at the point of the bayonet.

The necessity of defeating the attempt at revolution in Winnipeg is more apparent than ever, and the returned soldiers now fully realize that fact. Consequently, the Winnipeg trouble has entered on its final stage and the ultimate outcome is in no sense in doubt.

---

57 "AN APPEAL TO THE STRIKING SOLDIER"

The Telegram, Winnipeg
June 9, 1919

Soldiers who fought for your country; soldiers who fought for democracy; soldiers who fought for liberty; soldiers who fought for the defence and protection of women and children, but who are now engaged in the general strike, return to your true position in this community and dispel the confusion in the public mind that you have any sympathy with Bolshevism, any sympathy with revolution, or any sympathy with the traitors who are attempting to overthrow the very institutions in the defence of which you risked your lives.

You say that you are fighting for a principle today – and you must believe it or you would not say it. You say that you are fighting for a fair living wage, for the right of collective bargaining and for the restoration of all strikers to their former positions.

This may be your belief, this may be your conviction – but it is the belief of the vast majority of citizens of Winnipeg, of the vast majority of all returned soldiers, that whatever your intentions, the effect of your present attitude is to assist the men and women who betrayed you throughout the war, the men and women who are the blood relations of those men you fought in Europe; men and women who did everything possible to give aid and comfort to your enemies, and everything possible so to weaken your forces and your supports that you would perish miserably at the hands of the Hun.

The vast majority of the citizens of Winnipeg have no quarrel with you. They feel towards you only the kindliest sentiments, only the sincerest gratitude for the services you have performed. Even when you become confused in the public mind with men that the public despises, the people who are determined to stamp out revolution feel only sorrow, rather than anger, towards you.

The men and women whom you defended have good memories. They will never forget – but they feel hurt deeply to think that you believe that they are attempting to deprive you of either a fair living wage or any other right or reasonable privilege that you may require.

If you have a grievance, you can count upon the fair-minded people of Winnipeg, who are neither capitalistic exploiters nor trade unionists, to do everything to compel the removal of that grievance. The average man is just and grateful – and the average man so completely outnumbers the ingrate and the exploiter that with his backing you can get everything within the means of this community.

But no one can do anything to advance your interests, no one can assist you to the attainment of any end, so long as you participate in a general strike that was engineered by traitors, anarchists and Bolsheviks, who deliberately set out to overthrow the constituted authority for the preservation of which you fought – a general strike that finds the bulk of its support among the hostile aliens, who hate and despise you, but who by the treason of revolutionary union officials were admitted to the ranks of your unions while you were absent fighting for your country, and who now actually have the power of numbers in many unions to outvote you and to compel you to occupy a position that is inconsistent with all your traditions and that must be repugnant to your sensibilities.

Loyalty to your unions is to be commended; loyalty to your country is always commended. But remember that the first loyalty of all you returned soldiers should be to the cause for which you fought and to the comrades in arms who fought and died beside you.

Let no union brotherhood and no family ties break up your returned soldiers' organizations into rival groups that may, by some untoward incident, become bitterly hostile to each other. Remember the friendship cemented with blood – and then clean up your unions of the traitor and the foreigner, return peaceably to your positions and formulate any demands that you may justly ask for the amelioration of conditions that are admittedly hard, and ninety per cent. of the people of Winnipeg will use their every influence to see that you shall not ask in vain.

Dissociate yourself from any suspicion that you countenance treason, or that you have any sympathy with the attempt to paralyze this community for the benefit of the Hun and the Bolshevist, and then we can all join hands again as decent British subjects and work out our own destiny without the pernicious aid of the conspirator.

58 SOLDIERS AND STRIKERS

The Gleaner, Fredericton
June 9, 1919

The most significant incident of the strikes in the West is that demonstration at Winnipeg by a body of veteran soldiers who marched, 2,000 strong, to the City Hall to record themselves as militantly opposed to disorder, strikes and Bolshevism in general. And they meant business. One banner carried by the marchers said: "Down with Bolshevism. We uphold our duly elected constitutional Government." Another said: "To hell with the alien enemy: God save the King!"

It is grotesquely absurd to suppose that the returned soldiers have any sympathy whatever with the forces of disorder. The claim put forward in Toronto and elsewhere that the troubles were encouraged by disgruntled soldiers is a sheer bit of impudence. It is quite probable that the veterans will play a determining part in reconstruction, but they will not do it by violence or anarchy.

They are not yet fully organized, but the Winnipeg incident suggests how easily a compact machine can be put together. The material is ready; the men are used to disciplined, concerted action. The moment a leader appears they will follow, not merely in local but in national affairs. But he must be a real leader; one who not only understands and is one of them himself, but who is also a man of force and vision. The veterans are not trouble makers anywhere; rather, they are the soundest bulwark of the nation.

Section III

The Causes and Consequences of Violence,
June 10 – June 23

The R.C.M.P. disperse a mob of civilians, June 21, 1919.
[Published by permission of the Provincial Archives of Manitoba]

1 WAR HERO TRAMPLED BY ALIENS

The Manitoba Free Press, Winnipeg
June 11, 1919

Lying in a cot in Roblin hall at Tuxedo hospital is Sergt. Frederick George Coppins, V.C., who was attacked by a mob of striking aliens yesterday afternoon while performing his duties as a special mounted constable. Two bones on the right side of his chest are badly injured, but every hope is held for his recovery. He rested nicely throughout the night, and the doctors in attendance are entirely satisfied with his condition.

Sergeant Coppins was one of the first returned men to offer their [sic] services to maintain law and order in the city by joining the mounted constabulary, which has been organized by Major Dunwoodie.

Yesterday afternoon, with a number of his comrades, he was doing patrol duty on Main street south. Just north of the Industrial bureau was a hostile crowd of strikers, the majority of whom, it is stated, were aliens. Coppins became somewhat detached from the rest of the patrol, when a man, said to be a foreigner, ran forward to attack the horse. Coppins headed his steed toward the man, who managed to escape into the crowd.

From what can be gathered, the V.C. man was just turning his horse to rejoin the patrol when the animal was struck by a stone, which had been thrown from the centre of the crowd. The animal became unruly and Coppins, while endeavoring to pacify the beast, was dragged to the ground.

Immediately, according to his own story and that of eye-witnesses, he was set upon by a number of foreigners whom it is asserted kicked and jumped on the lad, who was badly injured before his comrades rode up to the rescue.

The spirit and pluck which resulted in the young soldier being decorated by his King with the greatest of all military honors, again manifested itself, and Coppins, although suffering considerable pain, and, with his right arm practically useless, again dashed into the fray.

2 WINNIPEG IS DISGRACED

The Telegram, Winnipeg
June 11, 1919

Yesterday Winnipeg was deeply disgraced. The worst riots ever witnessed in a Canadian city took place in our principal streets. Traffic was held up; private business was paralyzed; howling mobs held possession of the thoroughfares; thousands of bricks, stones, sticks and other missiles were hurled at the defenders of the law and human rights; scores were injured – some very seriously – and yet the Riot Act was not read!

It was the most painful and humiliating spectacle that any decent citizen could behold. Thousands of hoodlums defied and trampled on every principle of decency; trampled on the law; trampled on law-abiding citizens and their defenders – and yet the authorities of this city preferred to permit one of the finest bodies of heroic young men ever assembled together to be sacrificed to the persistent murderous assaults of hostile aliens, rather than to perform their obvious duty of employing immediately the full resources provided for such emergencies by the law of the land!

If yesterday's disgraceful riots did not justify the reading of the Riot Act and the immediate vigorous and complete suppression of the rebellion against constituted authority, then there is no occurrence that can be conceived when the reading of the Riot Act would be necessary.

Failure to read the Riot Act when it was most needed was merely the culmination, the climax, in a logical policy of temporizing, vacillating indecision that has encouraged the continuance of the strike for the past three weeks. We have been assured repeatedly that in such and such an event this and that would inevitably happen. The event has occurred – and a new assurance has been given as to what would happen if anything further should occur. The strike leaders and their alien followers, not unnaturally, have looked upon this policy of indecision as evidence of weakness. They have refused to believe that they would ever seriously be disturbed in carrying out their treasonable plans, even if they should go to the most extreme lengths.

What could be more natural? They have been repeatedly threatened with dire consequences, and the consequences have not ensued. It is perfectly reasonable, therefore, that they should assume that the authorities are bluffing. Consequently the citizens of Winnipeg must logically have expected to be compelled to witness the humiliating spectacles that they have witnessed – and they probably will not be surprised if they have to witness more.

What a thing to behold! One of the greatest heroes in the whole Empire dragged from his horse in the streets of Winnipeg and kicked to pieces by a mob of Huns!

What a thing to behold! Thousands of hostile aliens standing well back behind the crowds of British subjects and hurling thousands of missiles at the officers of the law – heroic young men who conducted themselves with a cool courage that has never been surpassed on the battlefields on which we made our sacrifices!

What a thing to behold! The representatives of the people, who are sworn to maintain the law, undertaking to assure us in these circumstances that the reading of the Riot Act was unnecessary, and following this up with dark hints of "extreme measures" to which resort would inevitably be made if anything more serious should occur!

It is painful to The Telegram to have to say these things. It is painful even to contemplate them. But no honest man and no honest newspaper, with proper appreciation of the facts and with a single-hearted desire to uphold the majesty of the law, can do anything but deplore in sorrow and indignation the lamentable failure of Mayor Gray and his advisers to discharge their obvious duty with a vigorous hand.

The inevitable crisis created by a policy of indecision arrived – and the Mayor failed to justify the enthusiastic support that has been freely and generously given by all classes of law-abiding citizens.

To blink this fact would not only be cowardly and dishonest, but it would also encourage further vacillation and indecision and neglect.

---

3 VICTORIA CROSS HERO ATTACKED IN STREET BY AUSTRIAN THUGS

The Tribune, Winnipeg
June 11, 1919

One of Winnipeg's greatest war heroes, a man who single-handed, charged a machine-gun nest and wiped out the crew, saving his platoon from annihilation, was struck down by Huns on the streets of Winnipeg Tuesday afternoon.

Sergt. F. G. Coppins, V.C., who returned to Canada a few weeks ago with the highest honors a British soldier can win, was dragged from his horse by alien ruffians, who, in typical Hunnish manner, kicked and trampled on him when he was down.

It is no fault of theirs that Sergt. Coppins is not dead today, a martyr to the cause of law and order.

One of Sergt. Coppins' ribs was broken, and two others severely bruised. He has every chance for recovery, however.

Coppins, himself, told friends who visited him at Tuxedo hospital today, that most of the men who attacked him were Austrians.

Only the timely interference of several of his companions, also on special policy duty, saved Sergt. Coppins from being trampled to death beneath the feet of the aliens. The police charged the crowd with swinging batons, and fought their way through to Coppins' side in time to save his life.

Coppins then attempted to rejoin his comrades. The crowd of aliens, which had gathered took this for an act of cowardice. Had they known Coppins' record for whipping Huns single-handed, it is a safe bet they would have followed their comrades' example and cried "Kamerad."

As the V.C. turned his back, a striker threw a stone which hit his horse. While Coppins was trying to regain control of the plunging beast, the aliens dragged him to the pavement.

Coppins was overwhelmed. His sole offence had been to volunteer to protect the lives and property of his fellow citizens. For that, the mob shouted for his life.

The war hero was knocked down, and aliens fought each other to be first in jumping on his chest.

It was a picture that would make Lenine and Trotzky [sic] laugh with glee – a British V.C. hero being mauled and trampled into the ground by Germans and Austrians.

Several mounted police fought their way through the crowd and dragged Coppins to his feet. The sergeant although his right arm was wrenched and bruised so badly that it hung useless at his side, dashed into the fray with his left hand, and gave as many of the aliens as he could reach a sample of the striking power of his one good arm. The Austrians would not fight, even with a one-armed man. That is not their style. They turned and made their way rapidly out of the crowd.

---

4 A RIOT BORN OF REVOLUTION

The Winnipeg Citizen
June 11, 1919

At the time of writing, Sergeant Fred Coppin [sic], Victoria Cross hero of France, is lying in the Military Hospital and is stated to be dying. He was not expected to live until morning. Sergeant Coppin swears that his injuries were caused by three Austrians who kicked him in front of Alloway & Champion's offices on Main street during the riot.

By the time that this appears, Coppin may be dead. Whether he is dead or alive; whether he lives or dies, the fact remains that he was kicked with intent to kill, by three Austrians – men whose blood relations he and every other returned fighter fought in France.

Coppin was dragged from his horse while he was fighting for democracy and British institutions just as truly as he fought for them overseas. The riot of yesterday was perpetrated and kept going by alien enemies, bent upon revolution and nothing else. These alien enemies are supported and were backed by British born men – and the

fact that those leaders are British born is sufficient to make every Briton hang his head in humiliation – who did their utmost to prevent Canada from taking her utmost part in civilization's battle for continued existence.

What under heaven do those returned soldiers who are on strike think of this outrage. Are Austrians, enemies of Canada, to be allowed to attempt to murder loyal soldiers, heroes, true Britishers, upon the streets of Winnipeg? Can any returned soldier countenance any continued affiliation with a gang of thugs and cutthroats?

This IS revolution, with a vengeance. This is THE revolution that has been planned for two years and brought to a head since January of this very year. This is the horrible thing that decent Trades Unionism has been tricked into – and this very rioting on the streets of Winnipeg was the effort of the Reds to commit all strikers to revolution, by violence, in a desperate effort to save the movement they had started from collapse and incidentally to save their own miserable hides as pretended leaders of the proletariat.

The revolution had failed without massed violence – therefore massed violence must be resorted to to save it; that is the psychology of the Bolshevist. This is the time of test. This is the time when all Trades Unionists – be they returned soldiers or not – must stand before the bar of their conscience and choose between anarchy, murder and blood on one hand; and ordered government, freedom, the Constitution and peace upon the other.

There is no middle ground. Let all this twaddle about "collective bargaining" drop in the face of bloodshed in the streets of Winnipeg. There is no middle ground between Sergeant Fred Coppin and the Austrian cowards who assaulted him with intent to kill.

Coppin, the hero, remained the hero. He was upholding British liberty and freedom as he rode in the saddle the protector of law and order. He won the Victoria Cross overseas; he fought for God, King and Country in the blood-soaked miasma of Northern France; and he had to fight for the salvation of a true Canadian democracy over there;

yesterday he was the embodiment, the personification of the British constitution itself and all that it stood and stands for – and in assailing Coppin, a peace officer and a Canadian V.C., three Austrian curs assailed that Constitution just as truly as the Kaiser himself assailed it in the fateful days of 1914.

One has not far backward to look for proof of revolutionary intent upon the part of the leaders of the present strike – who if Coppin dies are morally as guilty of his murder as are the curs who put the Prussianist boots to the hero yesterday.

On December 22, 1918 – less than six months ago – the leaders of the present strike – Alderman John Queen, Robert B. Russell, Sam Blumberg, William Ivens and F. J. Dixon called and addressed a revolutionary public meeting in the Walker theatre. That meeting was presided over by Alderman John Queen as chairman. That meeting sent greetings to the Soviet government in Russia and the Spartacans* in Germany. That meeting cheered declarations that revolution was coming in Canada and that blood would be spilled in establishing the dictatorship of the so-called proletariat.

*The Spartacans was the Bolshevik left wing in Germany which took its name from the leader of the slave revolt in ancient Rome. It became the Communist Party of Germany on January 1, 1919. [ed.]

5 "WHITE PEOPLE" AND ALIENS

The Herald, Calgary
June 18, 1919

That a Canadian soldier, the holder of the V.C., should have been kicked and crushed by Canadian residents and citizens on a Winnipeg street, is to the eternal disgrace of the men who are responsible for the striking conditions in Winnipeg. It is evident that the mob that thus maltreated a brave man was led by alien agitators, but one cannot help feeling surprised that the "white people" in the crowd, whether they sympathized with the strikers or not, per-

mitted such conduct and did not go to his defence. Surely those in Calgary and elsewhere who quit their work in sympathy with the Winnipeg trouble will see even more clearly now the character of the strike leadership and the sinister influences that are behind it.

6 THE ENEMY HERE IN CANADA

The Daily News Chronicle, Port Arthur
June 13, 1919

A man who was decorated with the highest and most honorable decoration within the gift of Britain, lies in a Winnipeg hospital with bones broken and flesh lacerated.

He received his injuries at the hands of three alien enemies on the public streets of that city. He received them while he was engaged in attempting to maintain law and order in a Canadian city.

Sergeant Coppin [*sic*] performed one of the most daring deeds of the thousands that are credited to individual soldiers in the great war.

The sole remaining man of a group of five who volunteered to destroy twenty-four hun machine gun nests, he won through and accomplished the task. Alone he fought one nest after the other, killing and wounding the huns who worked the guns. Terrified by the reckless bravery of this splendid hero those of the enemy who had not been killed surrendered.

By his heroic act he saved the lives of his comrades who were being destroyed by a murderous enfilading fire. He marched his prisoners back to the Canadian lines.

In the course of time Sergt. Coppin returned home. Imbued with the same spirit that urged him to his great deed over there, he volunteered as one of two thousand other soldiers to serve his city in its need, when the regular police refused longer to maintain law and order. It was in the discharge of this duty that he fell victim to the murderous assault of three alien enemies.

The assault was one of the most cowardly

acts that can be recorded. Thrown from his horse he lay for a moment on the ground unable to defend himself. It was while in this position that he was set upon and murderously stamped upon and kicked by the brutal aliens. His assailants escaped.

Alien enemies have taken an active part in every disturbance that has occurred at Winnipeg. It is time the authorities rounded up every man of alien blood who cannot show himself worthy of citizenship, and sent him back to the hovel from which he sprang.

It will be the solemn duty of Winnipeg to hunt out the three potential murderers and mete out to them that punishment which their crime merits.

Or is it to go down in the records that one of Canada's bravest men fell a victim at home to a murderous attempt on his life at the hands of the fellows of those whom he fought in France and Belgium, and his assailants were permitted to go free.

Sir Robert Borden utters brave words at Ottawa. Canadians and other loyal British subjects would like to see him put his words into execution.

7 THE INFLUENCE OF LOYAL VETERANS

The Standard, St. John
June 11, 1919

WESTERN CONDITIONS.

The attitude of returned soldiers in Winnipeg and other western cities toward alien labor agitators and unreasonable strike committees brings a new element into the situation, and one which will tend to create a wider confidence in the ultimate settlement of the difficulties now facing that part of the country. It is betraying no state secrets to say that authorities at Ottawa were as deeply concerned about the probable action of organized returned soldiers as of unionized labor, because of the fact that the country being so deeply indebted to these men could not deal harshly with them, but would in the very nature of things be called upon to make the greatest possible con-

cessions and to overlook, in the event of trouble, conduct which would not be permitted on the part of any others. Thus the stand which the soldiers have taken towards those who would disturb the even tenor of our national life, who would overthrow existing governments and attempt to take the law into their own hands, is a vote of confidence on the part of those soldiers in the fairness of Canada's administration and a further pledge of loyalty to the empire for which they fought. Apparently the feeling between the veterans and the alien labor leaders in Winnipeg, who have been successful to a certain extent in influencing organized labor there, is bitter indeed, and it is also clear that among the workers who went on strike on orders from the Central Strike Committee a very large number are now and have been anxious to return to work, but hesitate to do so solely through fear of molestation. Under guarantee of protection by the Winnipeg authorities, in co-operation with the soldiers who have volunteered for police duty, these workers are returning to their positions, and, while trouble may yet develop, it is pretty well recognized that the situation in Winnipeg has been due to the undesirable influence of persons who have not had the interests of labor at heart, but who have used organized labor for their own selfish purposes. . . .

8 LENINISM IN WINNIPEG

The Bulletin, Edmonton
June 12, 1919

Collective Bargaining Means Dictatorship of Wage-Earner.

According to Lenine's [*sic*] first annual report of his regime, industrial communism was only made possible of continuance in Russia by the adoption of a dictatorial directorship. A year's experiment showed that production "for the general good," instead of for wages and profit, could not be carried on. The workmen in the industrial establishments wouldn't work when they did not have to and production fell off.

Either Lenine had to "go," and Bolshevism collapse, or measures had to be taken to compel the unwilling workers to work. The piece-work system was introduced. The eight-hour day was made compulsory. "Disciplinary" shop rules were promulgated. And under these enforced conditions of employment the output of the factories was brought back to the volume of 1914.

The Bolshevik regime was saved from collapse, for the time, and the collective system of industrial control was given a pretense of practicability. But what of the Russian workman, who had murdered the boss and stolen his property under the delusion that he was thus paving the way for the establishment of a new industrial system in which he was to live in luxurious ease?

The position of that party to the transaction is naturally not depicted clearly in the dictator's resume. But it can be discerned from what is admitted. The piece-work system, the fixed eight-hour day, the "disciplinary" shop rules, make clear enough what the status of the workman is under the new order of things. He is simply a "cog in the industrial machine;" appointed to do certain work and a certain amount of it, and if he fails or refuses he does not eat.

The "democratization of industry" in Russia has thus led directly and quickly to the autocratization of industry, on the evidence of the head of the dictatorship. Instead of being a free man, entitled to leave a job that does not suit him for one that does, and to unite with his fellows in collective action to secure better conditions of labor, the factory operative is under absolute dictation of an irresponsible tyranny, which fixes his hours of labor, rates of pay and conditions of employment; and which enforces its orders with bayonets should they be disobeyed.

Individual liberty cannot exist under collectivism. The individual must be made to do what he is ordered to do, or communism is impossible. Lenine tried to operate a system of collective control of industry on a voluntary basis; failed, and was forced against his will to accept the methods of the dictator. The era of freedom which he and his deluded followers thought they were ushering themselves into was found in twelve months to be an era of industrial slavery. The free workman does not exist now under the Bolshevik regime. He is an industrial serf.

This not because the experiment was tried in Russia; but because the result must follow in the nature of things. The same course, adopted by any other people, would lead them to the same goal . . .

The sort of 'collective bargaining" that is now being advanced as one of the objectives of the sympathetic strikes that are keeping thousands of men in western cities from earning a living, is a species of collectivism, and leads in the inevitable direction. It is simply the Lenine system proposed in different language, and adapted to appeal to a different people. In essence and effect it is Bolshevism, and would produce the same effects upon the wage-earner and the public.

---

9 PROLETARIAN DICTATORSHIP

The Post, Regina
June 13, 1919

There are many citizens who hesitate to believe that anyone in Canada may actually be planning overthrow of the government by revolution. They doubt if anyone seriously believes that the democratic form of government that we have is unsatisfactory. They cannot understand that any one should wish to introduce conditions of anarchy into a reasonably prosperous country, in which there are unlimited opportunities for any man to lift himself out of the ranks of wage-earners; [*sic*] where there is practically no such thing as inherited wealth, and where practically every man has had to make his own way. These average citizens have ideas as to reforms which ought to be brought about. They desire to see profiteering wholly curbed and other wrongs righted. But the desire for revolution is something they cannot understand, and therefore they doubt that it exists.

Included in this number are many members of trades unions. Some of these have been led to vote for the "One Big Union" because it was presented to them in attractive colors, and because they have not taken the trouble to look behind this camouflage of "standing together" closely enough to see that anarchy is trying to ride into power on the shoulders of trades unionism.

For the doubters and for the dupes, the platform adopted by the "One Big Union" at its Calgary convention will repay study. It is not a theory that there are those in Canada who desire revolution. It is an admitted fact. It is not a theory either that the "One Big Union" is not a trades union movement, but a purely revolutionary plan. It is a fact in which the "One Big Union" glorifies.

The resolutions adopted by the "One Big Union" conference – the Western Canada Labor Conference at which the One Big Union received official sanction – include this: "Declaration of full acceptance of the principle of Proletarian Dictatorship as efficient for the transformation of capitalist private property to communal wealth."

The principle is Lenine's [sic] principle, and the words are Lenine's words. For about fifteen years Lenine has been the leader of the international European party supporting that view.

Read the words of that declaration. We may be sure they were not lightly chosen, but deliberately and carefully, so as to set forth with complete accuracy the meaning of the "One Big Union" movement. Note that they call first for a "proletarian dictatorship" to be used as an instrument for the abolition of private ownership of property. The "proletarian dictatorship" is the government (save the mark!) that exists in Russia today, or at least in those parts that are under the control of the Bolsheviki. It was proletarian dictatorship that ruled France in the days when Paris ran with blood, though in that instance the revolution was against autocracy. It is proposed in Canada as an antidote to the conditions of democracy!

The fact that the "One Big Union" conference sent 'fraternal greetings to the Bolsheviki and the Spartacan groups was seized upon by many as treasonable, and indignant protests were made. The greater significance of the program adopted for Canada was generally passed over, while, in reality, it constitutes the greater treason. The declaration is not merely a string of long words. It breathes a spirit which no loyal Canadian can accept.

The danger is that hundreds of labor men are thoughtlessly backing the "One Big Union" as a legitimate labor movement. It also constitutes a danger that so many citizens are willing to credit the statement that a revolutionary movement exists in Canada.

10 THE "PROLETARIAN DICTATORSHIP" IN WINNIPEG

The News, Nelson
June 16, 1919

Detailed reports of the happenings in Winnipeg only go to drive home the fact that the sympathetic strike organized by the One Big Union Bolshevist leaders in that city was nothing more nor less than an attempt to carry out a revolution and establish the soviet system of control of industries and government.

At the One Big Union convention at Calgary resolutions pledging support to the soviet system, the "proletarian dictatorship" and the Bolshevists in Russia and the Spartacans in Germany were passed. There was no attempt on the part of the One Big Union advocates to hide their intentions. They came out openly for revolution and Bolshevism.

When the strike began in Winnipeg it was declared by the One Big Union leaders that it was for the 44 hour week and "collective bargaining," but they soon showed their hand. One of the leaders is Rev. William Ivens. He is editor of the Western Labor News Strike Bulletin and has taken a leading part as spokesman for the strike leaders. He declared soon after the strike opened:

"Winnipeg is now governed by a soviet; the seat of authority has been transferred from the city hall to the labor temple.

"In a short time there would be no need to use the weapon of the strike. We shall not need to strike when we own and control industry – and we won't relinquish the fight until we do control."

The following extracts from the Strike Bulletin, the official organ of the strike leaders, show the extent to which it was attempted to usurp auhority [sic] and establish in Winnipeg the "proletarian dictatorship" to which the One Big Union convention at Calgary pledged itself:

"It is reported that certain rigs are delivering ice, bread, etc., without the printed cards authorized by the strike committe [sic] Some of them carry written notices. We warn all drivers that this is contrary to the orders of the strike committee."

"The police were asked to stay on the job so that there might be security. Men were requested to stay on the job and supply water sufficient for the homes of the people. Men engaged in the bread and milk industries were sent back to feed the people."

This is the "proletarian dictatorship" with a vengeance! Winnipeg babies were to get milk, Winnipeg homes were to get bread, Winnipeg people to secure water, Winnipeg police to remain on duty to maintain law and order, only under the control of the strike committee.

No wonder the mass of the people organized in support of the maintenance of constitutional democratic government and liberty.

11 THE RINGLEADERS SEIZED

The Times, Toronto
June 18, 1919

Leaders of the Winnipeg rebellion have been jailed, and must stand their trial on charges of sedition. The Federal Government collected evidence, while the featherheaded Strike Committee was issuing ukases and giving permits, and there is reason to believe that the men who have been seized will have a lot of explaining to do. In view of the fact that large sums of money have been expended on this continent by Lenine's [sic] agents to create industrial trouble and unrest, the Winnipeg dis-

turbance has had a suspicious appearance, from the beginning. The trial should be interesting.

We have no sympathy with the eternal argument for letting fools alone. Radicals always say that sharp action is bound to make the situation worse by rousing passion and causing overt acts of retaliation. They also declare that men placed under arrest on a political charge are likely to be hailed as martyrs. Those two arguments have been given undue weight by the British Government in the administration of Ireland. The result is a universal contempt for the weakness and vacillation of the authorities.

In Canada the Federal authority has never been sufficiently strong. It took a century, and a civil war to establish the Federal power of the United States in unquestioned dominance over the States on all Federal questions. The result is that Federal courts and Federal officers are respected. Bill Heywood, the Secretary of the I.W.W., is in jail. Eugene Debs is in jail. But neither is regarded as a martyr save by a few anarchists whose opinions are despised by the ordinary American citizen.

Surely the Government of Canada cannot forever tolerate unlawful and seditious activities, whether the offenders are capitalists or labor men, citizens or aliens, rich or poor. Every warning was given to the Winnipeg men. They were told publicly by a Cabinet Minister that they had been used by outsiders for revolutionary purposes. They had time and opportunity to "climb down" or else to get out of Winnipeg. They did neither. In apprehending them the Government is fighting the battle of the sane Labor leaders who from the first have denounced the sympathetic general strike as revolutionary in its methods and purposes. The simple fact is that the One Big Union is to-day the chief foe alike of regular Labor Unions and of constituted authority throughout the Dominion of Canada. We believe that the assertion of Federal power in this instance has been wise and timely.

12 STRONG ARM METHODS

The Albertan, Calgary
June 18, 1919

One day a local paper announces with approval that the "better element of Winnipeg, will not be satiated except by bloodshed." The blood of the laboring men was necessary before these people would rest in peace. Two days later it is announced that the government has placed several labor men under arrest, upon certain fanciful charges.

If there is bloodshed in this country, culminating in a catastrophe too awful to think about, the Canadian government which seems entirely dominated by the Winnipeg citizens' committee, must bear its share of the blame. The Winnipeg citizens' committee for the last few weeks has been using every possible effort to excite the labor men to some overt act and has been endeavoring to incite the returned soldiers to attack the laboring men. The Canadian government has stood behind the efforts of these people and has played into their hands.

The Winnipeg Free Press has been as vigorous as any other publicity agency in opposing the labor men. It has been unfair in its criticism and in its opposition. But extreme as it is, the Free Press disassociates itself from the "strong arm" methods adopted by the authorities. It realizes that this will complicate the situation and prolong and embitter the strike. The Free Press "emphatically disassociates itself from any strong arm policy of breaking the strike."

The Canadian government and the citizens' committee in Winnipeg are playing with a powder magazine. They are creating a serious and alarming situation in this country. They are dividing this country into classes, and creating a division which will exist for the coming generation.

The Calgary Herald is pursuing a similar course in this city. It asks that Ald. Broatch be punished and that action be taken. Such advice as this is not only unwise. It is dangerous. It borders on the criminal.

13 REASON FOR ARRESTS A SECRET

The Herald, Hamilton
June 18, 1919

WHY THE ARRESTS?

Inciting the Winnipeg police to neglect of duty is the formal charge made in the warrants authorizing the arrest of the ten strike leaders in Winnipeg yesterday morning. It appears that the charge is based on an article which appeared in the Western Labor News, the official Labor organ, attacking the special G.W.V.A. constables and calling them "thugs." But surely there must be some other basis for the charge. The published article might be sufficient reason for the prosecution of the responsible publisher or editor of the paper in which it appeared, or both of them; but it will probably be difficult to prove that all the men who have been arrested were responsible for it.

Hon. Gideon Robertson, minister of labor, is credited with the information that seized correspondence and documents show that the strike committee had been in receipt of "Bolshevik" money; also that a special committee had been appointed about a week ago to report on the feasibility of cutting off the city's supply of electric power. The latter piece of information has a sinister look; and yet it does not appear that any step was decided on. Merely considering whether it would or would not be expedient to cut off the power supply is not an overt act. Possibly the decision was against such a course. As for the receipt of "Bolshevik" money, surely no one will claim that as a just cause for the arrest of the strike leaders. No doubt they welcomed financial support from any quarter – probably would not have rejected it even if it had come from some capitalist source. The churches do not refuse to accept "tainted" money, and they justify their acceptance of it. It would be creating a new crime if the Winnipeg strike leaders were to be punished for accepting money contributed by Bolshevists.

It is not unlikely that the federal department of justice has acted on information which it deems inexpedient to make public at present. For that reason it is hardly fair to condemn the federal authorities just now for their action. Better wait and see what justification they have. The demands which have been made upon Sir Robert Borden by the metal trades council of Toronto for the immediate release of the arrested men, and other demands made upon the executive of the Dominion Labor congress for the calling of a general strike as a protest against the arrest, are unwise. Such demands are nothing less than attempts to interfere by intimidation with the administration of the law. It would be decidedly serious for Canada if such a course were to become popular.

What organized labor should demand is that the accused men shall be accorded a fair public trial by a jury of their peers, and that they be assured ample opportunity of defending themselves. Meanwhile it is not fair either to assume their guilt or to attribute sinister motives to the federal authorities.

14 ORDER, NOT REVOLUTION

The Telegram, St. John
June 18, 1919

It is revolution, not organized labor, at which the federal government has struck by the arrest of a dozen or more of the "Reds" who rose to leadership – to dictatorship – in the Winnipeg strike. If these are the men who preached sedition and who advocated and tried to carry into effect the overthrow of majority rule, the government's blow has fallen none too soon. The evidence upon which the action was based should be made known at once to the whole country. If it proves sedition and kindred offences, support of the government's course will be general, and strong. The country had impatiently awaited proof that the authorities would not tolerate revolution or the open advocacy of revolution in Canada. Unquestionably allies of "Reds" have been seeking to bring about what is called a proletariat dictatorship in the West, and if the men under arrest are among those guilty of such offences they should be placed upon their trial at once in order that the Canadian people may thoroughly understand the significance of the government's action.

The arrests follow a prolonged attempt to adjust the difficulties by moderate and conciliatory methods. Unfortunately this moderate policy was mistaken by the revolutionary element and their sympathizers for weakness and the hesitation of impotency. While the constituted authorities, civic, provincial and federal, sought to bring to an end the sympathetic strikes in Winnipeg and elsewhere by reasoned arguments and by concessions the leaders of the "one big union" scheme who were directing the revolutionary movement in the West, and who are said to have done so over the heads of a majority of the men in the craft unions, proceeded with their extreme designs. In fact, the resolute resistance of most of the people of Winnipeg had convinced these revolutionists that the ordinary strike methods would fail, had, indeed, failed, and they therefore sought to seize and exercise dictatorial powers by means of a general paralysis of industry and of all of the ordinary public activities in order that a minority might bring the whole community to its knees. The conditions which have led to federal intervention must be kept clear. The people of Canada for whom the government is acting, whose agent the government is, are not striking at organized labor or opposing themselves to the legitimate aims and aspirations of the craft unions, with which in fact they are much in sympathy, but through the government they are saying, and in no uncertain tone, that all who preach sedition, who abuse the liberty which this country guarantees them, who would place the "Red" flag and what it represents above the Union Jack and what it stands for, are public enemies and shall be treated as such. The men under arrest must answer the charge, not that they advocated or supported a strike, which it was their right to do, but that they advocated and carried on a movement designed to overthrow our existing institutions and set up a dictatorship which, if it succeeded, would give the whole country over to anarchy. As a

Winnipeg writer presented the matter a few days ago, these seditionists claimed the right "to plunge the whole community into confusion, to disrupt it, to bring it face to face with starvation, disease, and industrial impotence." "The citizens of Winnipeg," he declared, "will not lie down and die at the behest of the strikers. Neither will they submit to economic force majeure. That is the issue which has plunged this community into a very real form of war. The general sympathetic strike is a weapon directed at the throat of the whole body politic. Were it ever to be effective it would place one class in complete and absolute command of all others."

---

15 THE TRUE PURPORT OF THOSE ARRESTS

The Winnipeg Citizen
June 19, 1919

Now that certain men of pronounced revolutionary tendencies have been arrested upon charges of seditious conspiracy, certain sub-leaders of the revolutionary movement, together with the Socialist organ, are misrepresenting the reasons for the arrests and are asserting that the action of the authorities was a movement launched for the purpose of breaking the strike.

A labored effort is made by means of dark and mysterious hints to drag in the Citizens' Committee of One Thousand as having exercised some occult influence in the matter – of course, with a view to breaking the strike.

The persons interested in launching tirades against the authorities and against the Citizens' Committee know full well that their day is done the moment true organized labor is shown – as it can be and will be shown by documentary evidence – that organized labor has been used by Bolshevist revolutionaries as a means to revolution. Consequently, they are making desperate efforts to divert the issue and take attention away from themselves. Their desperation is evidenced by their attacks on the Committee of One Thousand – as though that body, or any other body aside from the govern-

ment itself could have taken or initiated the action that has landed eleven men in the penitentiary.

The undeniable fact of the matter is this: That the men arrested were not arrested because they were leading a strike; they were arrested for leading an attempt to start a nation-wide revolution, an attempt in which the betrayal of organized labor into a general strike was but the first stepping-stone.

They were arrested for the purpose, not of breaking the strike, nor any strike, but solely of preventing them from carrying out their revolutionary designs and to separate the strike from the revolution.

The arrests cannot successfully be distorted into an attack upon organized labor, for the move is in the interests of organized labor itself. Organized labor is always loyal to honest leaders, but once prove to organized labor that its leadership is dishonest and corrupt, once prove to organized labor that the men who have been trusted by them to lead have misused them for the revolutionary purposes of a Made-in-Germany anarchy, and labor will very speedily act in its own interests and restore the institutions of craft and brotherhood which it has taken whole lifetimes to upbuild.

There is no doubt that that proof will be forthcoming. The mere cursory, superficial preliminary examination of a few of the documents contained in the material obtained from the Labor Temple and other places under search warrant has revealed a real measure of that proof. And if a superficial examination of a few out of the carloads of documents has established so much, what may we not expect of the thorough examination of all of the seized documents?

The documents examined in but a casual glance into the pile have disclosed that R. B. Russell, business agent of the Metal Trades Council has, as secretary for the local branch of the One Big Union, been receiving Bolsheviki money from the Bolshevist organization in the United States, and that he has from time to time acknowledged the receipt of the funds. Thousands upon thousands of honest workpeople on strike would utterly refuse to believe that

Bolshevism is behind this Winnipeg situation – without being given just the concrete evidence that Russell's receipts provide.

If collective bargaining were the only issue and not a mere pretext, why was not the sympathy strike called off when the collective bargaining issue was settled to the satisfaction of all the tenets of organized labor?

If anything were ever needed in this country it was the arrest of those men, in order that the truth might be revealed to true Organized Labor and true Organized Labor thus provided with the opportunity to rehabilitate the Trades Union movement; and to restore it to its previous position of confidence and respect in the community.

---

16 THE ARRESTS

The Herald, Calgary
June 19, 1919

Quite a number of well-meaning people are apt to confuse the issue with respect to the arrest of the Winnipeg strike leaders. Such confusion is greatly aided by a newspaper like the Calgary Albertan, which strives to make the arrest an issue in the labor conflict.

The arrest of the Winnipeg strike leaders has nothing whatever to do with the issues in the strike. These men are arrested, just the same as any other suspected criminals would be arrested, charged with breaking the laws of Canada. If they are guilty, they deserve no sympathy from anyone, and The Herald believes will get as little sympathy from labor as from anyone else. If they are innocent, they should, and no doubt will, be promptly released and can resume their strike activities or not, as they please.

To say, as the Albertan does, that because they have been remanded for a week the country may be thrown into a general strike is absurd and with the Albertan the wish is father to the thought. The board that will try them is on its way from Ottawa. Both prosecution and defence have a right to reasonable time for preparation. If they had

been summarily tried and deported, the Albertan would have been the first to claim that they had been "railroaded."

Remember that these men are accused of endeavoring to upset constitutional government in Canada, and of receiving money from outside this country in order to carry out that design. Until their offence is proved they must be considered innocent, but it would be just as reasonable to prejudge them and say they are guilty as it is to prejudge the government and say it is guilty for having arrested them. The case is in the hands of the law. It would be better to leave it there without comment or agitation until the scales of justice have been properly balanced.

---

17 THE WINNIPEG MARTYRS

The Telegraph, Quebec
June 20, 1919

THE LABOR CRISIS

The move of the Government in arresting the Winnipeg strike leaders has undoubtedly provoked a serious labor crisis throughout the whole Dominion. Even among those who disapprove most strongly of the One Big Union movement, with its first cousins Bolshevism and revolutionism, there is, nevertheless, a strong feeling that the Government in resorting to the mailed fist doctrines has made avowal of an active hostility to labor generally. And labor movements cannot be suppressed by violence and repression. In the last analysis, it is only the public opinion of a democratic people that can prevail in such a country as Canada.

There is no doubt that seditious Bolshevist agitators should not be allowed to operate in Canada. Undesirable immigrants of this ilk should be quietly weeded out by the secret police and deported to the lands from which they come. But that is a different matter from clumsily arresting a group of strike leaders at a time when the eyes of the whole country are upon them, and when only a week or two since, the Government representatives were negotiating with them on a basis of absolute recognition of their movement. And now it cannot be said that it is really because of their seditious utterances that they are in prison. It is because they were behind the Winnipeg strike.

As a result, they have become martyrs. The common sense of good Canadian labor that will have nothing to do with their theories or their methods, is, nevertheless, irritated at the brute force system being employed by the Government. Once more the Ottawa authorities have shown themselves strangely obtuse and inept in dealing with a delicate situation which required strength without violence, and restraint without weakness.

Mounted Police holding Main Street just after the riot, June 21, 1919.

[Published by permission of the Provincial Archives of Manitoba]

"Bloody Saturday," June 21, 1919.

[Published by permission of the Provincial Archives of Manitoba]

18 A FAIR TRIAL

The Chronicle, Halifax, N.S.
June 23, 1919

Whatever may be said as to the wisdom or unwisdom of the action taken by the Government in arresting a number of the Winnipeg strike leaders on the charge of sedition, it is certainly well advised in allowing them to be released on bail, prior to a fair and open trial by due process of law. The manner in which the arrests were effected tended to create an unfavorable impression among many who disapproved of the strike methods in Winnipeg, and it had the inevitable effect of antagonizing organized labor throughout the country and of adding new bitterness to the dispute, which, according to the Winnipeg Free Press, was on the eve of settlement.

Every Canadian worthy of the name will support constitutional and legal measures taken to suppress sedition and maintain law and order. But the liberty of the subject must not be impaired. It must be maintained inviolate as it is now inviolable under the British constitution. As the Toronto Star points out, adverse public opinion can be overcome only by a fair trial and by the clearest evidence. Having invoked the aid of the courts, the Star urges, the Dominion Government, which is responsible for the action, must take more than usual care to provide for a fair trial before an impartial tribunal. Wher [sic] men are charged with seeking to overturn the institutions of the country, and when the aim of the authorities is to vindicate and defend those institutions, everything must be done to maintain public confidence in them. It must be made clear that what is sought is simply justice, justice to the defendants as well as to the community at large. To quote the Star:

"There must be scrupulous regard for the liberty of the subject, and for his right to all the safeguards erected by British law. The trial must be so solemn and deliberate, so free from prejudice and passion, as to impress the public and inspire confidence. Nothing of course can be said as to the merits of the case until the evidence is produced. If it is strong enough not only to convict but to convince the authorities will be vindicated, and will have gained their point. If the evidence is weak the authorities will be discredited, and the situation altered for the worse. The strikers will be embittered by what they will regard as persecution and unfair use of the arm of the law; and organized labor will regard the instigators of the proceedings as enemies of its cause. All this, we must suppose, has been carefully weighed. The proceedings will be watched with the utmost interest. They will constitute a great State trial, and they should be dignified, deliberate, and scrupulously fair."

It must be assumed that before taking such a drastic step the Government authorities had discovered evidence of seditious conduct on the part of the accused, which warranted them to be placed under arrest. If such evidence exists, there is a right way to produce it; it is in open court. Trial by jury is a cardinal principle of British justice. It is the inalienable right of every British subject. The lowest criminal in the land is entitled to a fair and open trial, and it is gratifying now to learn that the authorities have taken this view and that the charges will be investigated fairly and properly in a constitutional way.

---

19 WHO WAS RESPONSIBLE?

The Albertan, Calgary
June 23, 1919

THE WINNIPEG RIOT

The tragic climax of the disturbance in Winnipeg, though lamentable in the result, was neither surprising nor unexpected. The nature of the exact incident which led to the outbreak may be questioned, but the public in a crisis of this kind, when recognised [sic] authority is set at defiance, must side with law and order. Now that the trouble has reached this stage of terror, the mayor of Winnipeg and his associates must be firm in their effort to maintain the peace. Upon that one point there will be little difference of opinion, however much there may be a variance as to the underlying causes that led up to this deplorable event.

The mayor of Winnipeg a few days ago, quite properly put the ban upon all street processions. That was a wise precaution to preserve order and prevent the outbreak which threatened whenever there was any considerable demonstration by either party in this labor war. The strike sympathizers apparently violated this reasonable precaution. The mayor gave sufficient warning that he would use every means in his power to enforce his mandate and preserve order. This warning was not observed, and the violation of the order led up to the tragic occurrence.

Whether the police used their authority without discretion, or whether some person in the crowd precipitated the crisis, does not seem clear. But in an event of this kind, with the atmosphere electrically charged as it was little was necessary to ignite the spark and set aflame the passions of the excited crowd.

Unfortunately the people of Winnipeg had been prepared for an event of this kind. For some weeks both parties seem to have anticipated an outbreak in the end. Newspapers have been carrying large notices of an incendiary nature, which could have no effect other than to fan the flame. Newspaper correspondents in Winnipeg have been calmly informing the outside public that the better class of Winnipeg people demanded blood and would be satisfied with nothing less. With feeling running so high, the outbreak was not surprising.

The representatives of the Canadian government from the beginning seem to have aggravated the trouble rather than have pacified it. When they arrived in Winnipeg they found two parties lined up if not in battle array, certainly in battle humor. Instead of declining to deal with either party and summoning moderates from the two sides, the cabinet ministers seem to have thrown their entire influence and strength with the extremists opposing the strikers. Under such circumstances it is not surprising that they made little headway.

Following this outbreak we shall hear much now about the red rebels of Winnipeg, and the Bolshevists who will be charged with the uprising. To what extent this charge of Bolshevism can be made against the strike leaders will be known when the evidence is produced in the court trial of the men under arrest which will soon be held. But even if the men are found guilty of sedition and illegal acts, and punished as they deserve, the government will have done but little to solve the labor unrest which certainly does exist. In Canada as in all other countries the heart of labor unrest is to be found in the insistent claim not only to better conditions of living but to vitally different status for the worker. In Canada as elsewhere the Bolshevik leader cannot engineer a grave movement of industrial revolt unless there is a mass of genuine industrial unrest on which to build.

The riot of Saturday is a worrying and deplorable incident which cannot have but evil results whatever may be the ultimate outcome of the whole distressing disturbance, and makes more difficult all efforts looking toward permanent labor peace.

The incident will injure the labor faction most, which up to this time has shown much self-control and patience under very great provocation.

The Albertan believes that the Canadian government, particularly the minister of labor, by his tactless manner, and his clumsy methods is to some considerable extent responsible for the long delay in the settlement of the strike which had its terrible climax on Saturday last.

However, the public which is now fully aroused is most interested in seeing law and order preserved, and will take any reasonable action to assist the authorities in preserving peace. When labor peace comes the public will then consider fully the errors of the men in responsible positions.

20 FRUITS OF REVOLT

The Mercury, Estevan, Sask.
June 26, 1919

Winnipeg has at last tasted blood and is satisfied. A couple of mortals have been passed on to where there is no industrial unrest, a hundred more are limping around with bullet wounds, and the unscarred thousands are content to resume again their former relations as employer and employed, exploiter, worker and consumer. This is the second experience that Winnipeg has had with restless spirits who would upset established law and usher in a new dispensation. Louis Reil [sic] dreamed his dream of a new empire of the plains and attempted to give it substance and finality by spilling blood. He failed in his purpose, but out of the killing of Thomas Scott issued drastic reforms in the administration of affairs in Western Canada that made possible a new empire greater than Riel ever conceived. So will it be following the tragic events of the past week. The blood spilled on the streets of Winnipeg will not bring about Soviet government, but it has sealed the doom of those who would go whoring with the God-given rights of people to live by the fruits of their own labor.

It is eighty years since William Lyon MacKenzie [sic], goaded to desperation by the insolence of privilege and the burden of established injustice, raised the flag of revolt in Canada. He did not succeed in overthrowing British government: on the contrary, he compelled reforms that made possible the building of a yet greater Britain whose foundation lies deep in the hearts of its people.

So will it be with the Winnipeg strike, and the strikers, and all those who did not strike but suffered. The administration has been jarred into activity and must find remedy for rampant evil. Predatory privilege has become alarmed and will make peace with the masses. And at that the spilled blood will have been well spilled.

Section IV
Postmortem

1 THE WINNIPEG DEADLOCK

The Globe, Toronto
June 17, 1919

Now that Bolshevism has been defeated in Winnipeg, and the supporters of law and order have secured definite control of the city, an effort should be made to obtain a settlement of the fundamental points of difference between Labor, Capital, and the citizens, who, although interested neither as employers nor workers, were the principal sufferers from the general strike.

With Bolshevism there can be no compromise, but nothing is to be gained by an attempt to destroy trade union organization in Winnipeg. The situation that exists there has arisen not because of but in spite of Labor organization. The leaders of long-established unions, such as the railway running trades federation, have been most conservative, and have done much to lessen the tension. They have sought earnestly but without result to bring about a settlement of the metal trades dispute. They report that the employers still stand out for the open shop and against the recognition of the Metal Trades Council as the proper body to represent the workers in collective bargaining.

At this distance that looks like a mistaken attitude on the part of the employers. In Great Britain the masters are accepting frankly and unreservedly the principle that the workers should have the widest right of choice as to the representatives to be entrusted with negotiations on their behalf. For the most part the British Industrial Councils are organized on a "one-industry" basis, the Councils being first chosen by the shop employees, then by districts, and lastly to represent the industry in its national aspect. It is extremely doubtful whether any representative body of British employers would refuse to sit down at a table for the purpose of bargaining with members of such a body as the Metal Trades Councils of Winnipeg and of Toronto. Such Councils would assuredly see to it that moulders would be delegated to speak and bargain for moulders, machinists for machinists, and blacksmiths for blacksmiths. It cannot be said that a Council so organized is unrepresentative, or that the employers are asked to deal with Labor delegates who are ignorant of the conditions in the trade.

Among unprejudiced Winnipeg business and professional men there is a feeling that the public interest ought not to be placed in jeopardy by a continuation of hostilities between the metal workers and their employers over a point of difference that should be capable of settlement by conciliatory methods. This view was voiced by Canon Murray of St. John's Cathedral when he urged on Sunday that the Labor troubles of Winnipeg be ended by "frank acceptance of collective bargaining in the full sense in which practically everyone in England now accepts it, which would include a Metal Workers' Council," and on the other side frank recognition that sympathetic strikes should not extend to police, firemen, and the city's light and water employees. Canon Murray proposes that these two conditions be agreed upon as the basis of a general settlement in Winnipeg. There is no sign as yet that the Citizens' Committee is bringing influence to bear upon the employers to accept the Metal Workers Council as Labor's representative in collective bargaining. The Citizen, the paper published specially to represent the views of the people of Winnipeg who are against sympathetic strikes, says that "collective bargaining never was challenged; the only dispute as to that was as to whether employers should bargain with an outside organization not composed of employees, and who claimed the right to control all the employees in all the shops."

Is there enough of a difference here to warrant a continuation of industrial strife in Winnipeg and Toronto, accompanied by sympathetic strikes in many other widely separated parts of Canada? The average man who is neither a metal worker nor a metal manufacturer believes that Canada is being kept in a turmoil largely on a point of order. The crushing of Bolshevism has been accomplished. The Dominion will have none of the Russian nostrum. But the energy and the fine ideals of the citizens of Western Canada ought not to be enlisted in a war upon trade unionism because a relatively small proportion of the union workers of the country have despised and flouted the advice of their responsible leaders, and have tried unsuccessfully the short cut of the One Big Union. The Winnipeg deadlock ought not to be allowed to continue indefinitely. Bolshevism having been defeated, Labor and Capital engaged in the metal trade should sit down and do business by collective bargaining as they do in many other industries and in many other cities.

2 NO 'HAIRY BOLSHEVISTS' IN WINNIPEG

The Herald, Montreal
June 25, 1919

The Winnipeg strike, which has lasted six weeks, is to end to-morrow. The principle of the sympathetic strike, or general strike, or one big union, whatever it may be called, has received its death blow in Canada, if Winnipeg is to be the applied test. The idea is industriously propagated in certain quarters that the trouble in Winnipeg was due to the foreign element and Bolshevik money. The idea of Soviet government is by no means confined to Russia and Hungary. It is an outcrop of Socialism among the many brands you prefer. But the strike leaders in Winnipeg were all British born. The six strike leaders arrested by order of the Federal Government and taken to the penetentiary [*sic*] fourteen miles out of Winnipeg, and now out on bail to stand trial in a few days, were: R. B. Russell, William Ivens, Ald. John Queen, Ald. A. A. Heaps, George Armstrong and R.E. Bray. Five men of alien birth were arrested at the same time, but for them its a question of whether they should be deported. To argue that the well-organized labor unions of one of the most progressive cities of the Dominion were led and controlled by some hairy Bolshevists is to insult every labor unionist in Canada. To prove that Mr. Russell received a letter from the United States offering him Bolshevik money is nothing. Lenine is shoving out money all over the world by the barrel, and the surprise would be that Russell received only one such letter. Organized labor in Winnipeg would have plenty of money of its own to use for what is considered the interests of its membership.

It has been publicly declared more than once that Great Britain is a field ripe for Bolshevik operations and it is a significant fact that the present visit to America of J. H. Thomas, M. P., an aggressive member of the labor group in Great Britain, was to organize an international strike movement that would tie up the transportation of two continents, according to the published statement of one of his colleagues in New York, where Thomas has been working in secret for some weeks. In Canada there is no field for Bolshevists or Reds. We must be on guard against the propaganda, which is quite active, but that does not mean that in a kind of panic we should ascribe every strike in the Dominion to aliens and Bolshevists. Of the fifteen men who compose the strike committee in Toronto eight were born in England, two in Scotland, four in Canada and one in Russia.

3 WINNIPEG DEFEATS BOLSHEVISM

The Telegraph, Kitchener
June 28, 1919

Bolshevism has been defeated in Winnipeg. The calling off of the Winnipeg strike and the return to work of the metal workers as well as those who went out in sympathy, marks the complete failure of a seditious conspiracy that has paralysed business at the Manitoba capital for the past six weeks. While the municipal, provincial and Dominion authorities were slow in putting the arm of the law into motion against the band of revolutionaries in the guise of labor leaders that dominated the general strike committee, when the blow fell it came with a dramatic force that spelt the beginning of the end of the General Strike Committee's regime which ended in unconditional surrender a few days later.

The result should not be interpreted as a

defeat for labor honestly seeking its just rights. Thousands of those who went out in sympathy returned to work when they realized they had been duped by their would-be friends of the Central Strike Committee. The result is rather a victory for the forces of law and order in Winnipeg, and serves notice on all and sundry, that Bolshevism will not be tolerated in Canada.

---

4 PROFITEERS AND BOLSHEVISTS

The Globe, Toronto
June 26, 1919

The end of the Winnipeg sympathetic strike will be welcomed by all but the few who seek to turn Labor troubles into revolutionary propaganda.

The outcome should give special satisfaction to trades unionists. The strike was engineered by their enemies in furtherance of the One Big Union, the Canadian counterpart of the I. W. W. Thousands of trades unionists who answered the call of the Strike Committee from a mistaken idea of loyalty to fellow-workmen have been loath to believe that they were being used to undermine the crafts unionism which is the basis of the great international Labor organizations, but they have had their eyes opened to the real nature of the conspiracy. The junta which promoted and directed the strike was not concerned about higher wages and shorter hours, or even collective bargaining. These specific demands made a plausible excuse for appealing to the rank and file, but the "Reds" who acted as leaders were interested only in fostering a spirit of revolt and in getting more power into their own hands. Their newspaper at the outset of the strike let the cat out of the bag by proclaiming a Soviet Government in Winnipeg. A member of the committee, in acknowledging the receipt of Bolshevist money, boasted also that they had "killed the Labor party." Their revolutionary aims were so apparent that the majority of the strikers had returned to work before the committee bowed to the inevitable by calling the strike off.

One of the compensations of the strike has been the arousing of a community sentiment. The impudence of the Strike Committee in presuming to control public utilities and usurp the functions of civic government was a challenge which citizens of all classes accepted. Their impromptu organization to maintain municipal services and the distribution of foodstuffs showed the would-be Soviet that it had gone too far. Any group that tries to dictate to any Canadian community will meet with the same response.

The comparative calm which will follow the wave of sympathetic strikes should be used by trades unionists to get a firmer control of the Labor movement. If employers are wise they will aid in suppressing the revolutionary elements by establishing closer relationships with the responsible Labor organizations, admitting them to a larger share in their councils and in the rewards of industry. And they will regard the profiteer in their own ranks as an enemy as menacing as the Bolshevist.

---

5 LABOUR'S LOSSES

The Gazette, Montreal
June 26, 1919

THE STRIKE COLLAPSE.

The first great effort in Canada to apply the One Big Union idea has ended in a failure, the biggest that has overtaken organized labor in this country. Six weeks ago, in the hope of helping certain metal workers who had quit their places to compel their employers to accede to their demands, the Winnipeg Trades and Labor Council ordered a general strike. The extent to which the order was obeyed was remarkable. Postal and civic services were disrupted, the street railway was stopped from operating. Efforts were made to tie up the general railway system. The distribution of foodstuffs was put under an interdict. Many industries and activities which had nothing to do with the original dispute were interrupted. Like interruptions of industry were ordered at Edmonton and Calgary, Vancouver, Victoria and other places. The different trades and labor councils acted with all the tyranny of the Russian Soviets. Their leaders may or may not have had it in their heads to revolutionize the system of government of Canada. Some of their acts, however, suggested that they thought they were strong enough to do what they pleased. They ignored the public convenience; they held up some of the greater governmental services; they openly defied the established authorities and the law for the preservation of public order. The first effect of such a policy was to turn public opinion against the strike, its leaders and all connected with its maintenance. The moral influence of public opinion, which generally favors "labor," was turned against those who represented labor in the struggle; and that was the beginning of the end. Private employers were encouraged to stand out and compel a collapse of such a tyrannous organization. Government and municipal authorities were applauded when they announced that the staffs which had causelessly left their employment were formally dismissed. Outside of Winnipeg the sympathetic strikes were weak and began to fail as soon as they were ordered. Now the Winnipeg one has broken down. It is well that such should be the case. The transportation and industrial activities of Canada would be gravely endangered if, even for a time only, small trades and labor councils representing only a minority of the workers, could, at their will, paralyze the trade and public services of a large part of the country, and cause the loss of millions of properly invested capital on the free employment of which practically all labor depends. This is now seen so clearly that it is hardly necessary to point it out. It is likely to be long before there is an effort to repeat the Winnipeg strike on such a scale. The rank and file of labor has lost so heavily by following the advice of unwise counsellers [sic] that the steady thinking men should have for a long time a better chance to assert themselves.

6 NOT A DEFEAT FOR UNIONISM

The Times, Victoria
June 25, 1919

THE END OF THE STRIKE.

After inflicting enormous loss upon the country, occasioning much hardship for thousands of innocent people in no way directly involved in the particular dispute out of which it arose, and causing violent death and bloodshed, the sympathetic strike in Winnipeg has come to an end without a single aspiration of those who instigated it being realized. The men who sought to utilize the tie-up as a means of overthrowing constituted authority and erecting a soviet government, and who, by obtaining control of the machinery of organized labor were able to delude a large number of workers the majority of whom are absolutely sound at heart, into following them up to a certain point, now are awaiting trial for sedition. Millions of dollars have been lost in wages by those who went on strike, many have lost their positions and are confronted with an unpromising outlook for the future, the harmony which had existed between employers and employees in many industries for years has been ruptured, leaving bitterness and distrust, and there is nothing to show for it all. Even the issue in the metal workers dispute remains unsettled.

The defeat of the sympathetic strike, however, is not a defeat for the trades unionist movement. As we have pointed out time and again, no principle of recognized trades unionism was involved. The heads of labor unionism in America, the men who have directed organized labor for years, who have helped it to achieve its fine record for mutual betterment, were sternly and relentlessly against the strike. They knew it for what it was – a deliberate attempt planned in Calgary to wreck the trades unionist movement and set up the Red oligarchy denoted by the "One Big Union" idea. They realized that if it had succeeded organized labor would have been severed from its international connection and the source of its chief strength and protection, with the result that ultimately it would have been left at the mercy of the exploiter.

The strike, thus, was largely a fight between the promoters of the "One Big Union" and sane trades unionism and, therefore, one of the chief factors in its defeat was the attitude of the leaders of the great international organizations and the steadfast support given to them by the members of the unions throughout the country who declined to join the extremist movement. If the outcome of the trouble will result in the elimination from its ranks of the apostles of Lenine and Trotzky [*sic*] who temporarily have managed to control its local machinery in many instances, organized labor in Canada will emerge stronger, more influential and a more effective agency for public good than it ever has been before.

Organized labor has a great opportunity before it. Never was there a time in the history of the country when a fair and sound presentation of its case for the improvement of economic conditions was more certain of hearty support than now; the great neutral populace has no more use for the profiteer than it has for the anarchist. A readiness to co-operate with all other elements for the promotion of the public good, to proceed along reasonable, constitutional lines in effecting necessary reforms never fails to enlist the goodwill of the public. The Bolshevist, extremist or Maximalist programme never can succeed in Canada. Force, threatening the basic governmental institutions of the country only begets crushing, superior force on the other side. Those institutions are not perfect; far from it. But they are, at least, as perfect as the public whose mental, moral and political processes they reflect. And they are a thousand times more perfect than the products of anarchy and chaos.

7 THE LESSONS TO BE LEARNED

The Star, Montreal
June 26, 1919

THE END OF THE WINNIPEG STRIKE.

The decision of the Winnipeg strikers to abandon the "sympathetic" strike which for the past six weeks has nearly paralyzed the city was inevitable from the moment when it became apparent that an appeal to force on the part of a certain element among the strikers was a failure. A further continuance of the deadlock was impossible to both employers and employed, and the fatal riot of last Saturday was the logical termination of the attitude taken by the least responsible of the agitators.

It is too soon to estimate what the strike has cost the city in money. It will run into hundreds of millions of a loss which will have to be borne by all classes of citizens, by the strikers equally with the employers, and by a great majority of the citizens who are neither. One man was shot dead during the rioting of Saturday, two others died of injuries received, and many are still in the hospitals. Possibly other deaths could be indirectly traced to the effects of the strike upon the very young and the very old. It will be a long time before the consequences of the last six weeks will be effaced.

It is no part of The Star's Business to discuss the cause of the Winnipeg outbreak. That is a matter for the people of Winnipeg and the Government authorities, provincial and federal, to settle for themselves. But it is impossible to misunderstand the significance of the result. The majority of the Winnipeg strikers had no real grievances of their own for which to fight. Group after group went out, not because they themselves had anything to complain of, but because they believed themselves to be aiding other workingmen who had. There might have been general understanding of this action had it not, in many cases, been taken in direct violation of pledges given by the "sympathetic" strikers to their employers.

It was pointed out at the time what the consequences of such action would inevitably be, and the breakdown of the general sympathetic strikes proves what should have been evident to the strike leaders from the beginning. It does not pay to treat agreements as "scraps of paper." That is what certain of the Winnipeg strikers did, and that action cost them the sympathy and understanding of the public. It enlisted against them the great masses of the citizens, and it was from the volunteer organizations formed from these that the city's essential services were carried on. If the strike proves anything, it proves that good faith is the best asset of either employer or employe and that, lacking that fundamental, neither can prosper.

Some of the strikers, by their action, have made it impossible for their former employers to reinstate them, but the majority, badly led, as The Star believes they were, will be wiser now than they were before they listened to foolish counsel. The Winnipeg strike, serious as it has been and grave as its consequences will be, will not have been an unmixed evil if it teaches both sides the sanctity of agreements.

---

8 GENERAL STRIKES MUST ALWAYS FAIL

The Evening Mail, New York
July 2, 1919

The general strike at Winnipeg has failed even more completely than did its predecessor of some months ago at Seattle. It lasted for more weeks than the Seattle strike did for days. It has ended in the complete surrender of the workers with nothing to show for their effort but a record of hardship and semi-starvation endured in the vain following of a chimera.

The idea of the general strike as a weapon for labor to use originated with the more or less philosophical French anarchist Sorel. But Sorel had no hallucinations as to the effectiveness of the weapon. His Gallic mind was too shrewd and logical for that. He himself described it as the necessary myth with which to hypnotize the minds of discontented. He was in the position of the religious fakir who misleads people with a hypocritical promise of the kind of Valhalla their appetites desire.

But for hundreds who know the theory of the general strike as Sorel preached it, there are few who know that he called it "the necessary myth." And so, when the half-baked orators of revolution got among discontented workers and, for quick results, they were able at Winnipeg and Seattle to mislead the crowds.

There is a fundamental reason why the general strike must always fail under present conditions of industry, when it is resolutely opposed. That reason lies in the fact that the worker or producer is also a consumer. When he ties up the general processes of all industry, he is tying up his own food supply. Until he can become the producer of his own needs the general strike is bound to fail.

---

9 A UNITED STATES VIEW OF THE STRIKE

The Courier, Buffalo
July 4, 1919

The big strike in Winnipeg and other cities of the Canadian Northwest was called off yesterday. The strikers do not even gain compromises.

Thus the second attempt to start a Bolshevist movement on this continent has failed. The first one was the strike at Seattle.

The persons who have rushed to the front as Bolshevists have little chance on this side of the Atlantic and are little to be feared. The greater danger of Bolshevism now lies in the gradual adoption of its ideas by other leaders who are in the regular organizations. Communism, redivision of property and political control of government by a special labor class have certain attractions as theories, particularly for those who would expect to be at the front and to share in the personal power and profit of such a revolution. Any revolution necessarily makes great men and usually rich men of those who are able to lead it and they do not always need even to win in order to secure some of these personal rewards.

It is against this sort of insidious encroachment of Bolshevism that the people need most to beware. They have only to study Russia honestly in order to learn that this kind of government brings only suffering and horror for the mass of common people, whatever it may do for the leaders.

10 GENERAL STRIKES ARE FUTILE

The New York Post
June 26, 1919

After almost six weeks the Winnipeg strikers have gone back to work, with no more to show than the appointment of an investigating commission. Considering the bitterness aroused and the sacrifice involved, it will be difficult to call this anything but a defeat for the purposes of the strikers, whatever those purposes were. And it is still more a defeat because the unions failed to make quite clear what they wanted. The background of the trouble – the conference of labor in Western Canada which declared for one big union and voted a general strike in favor of a thirty-hour week and the restoration of civil liberties – had an unmistakably revolutionary tinge. Its aims seemed in large measure political. All these aims were not avowed when the Winnipeg and other unions went out. The leaders stated, again and again, that they wanted higher wages and the right of collective bargaining in a new sense – that is, bargaining not between a single union and its employers, but between a group of unions and the employers. This was only a short step towards the "one big union," but it failed to be taken.

M. Jaurès, the murdered French Socialist leader, long ago wrote a penetrating analysis of the general strike as a revolutionary weapon. Let us concede, he said, that enough workers in strategic positions down tools so that the necessary processes of the nation are stopped. What then? Either the strike must succeed quickly or it is doomed to miserable failure. The strikers themselves will have to surrender along with the rest of the population. They injure themselves as much as any one else. Furthermore, the hardships they cause will set the public against them. If what they intend is a violent seizure of power, the strike merely strengthens popular support of the authorities. The strikers cannot win, either quickly or in the end, unless preponderant public opinion is with them. But if the public is with them, would the strike be necessary, except in an autocracy? As a threat, said Jaurès, or as a brief demonstration, the general strike may be effective, but as a means of revolution it is bound to fail.

The tactics of the general strike now include one element left out of consideration by Jaurès. Certain exemptions are made, so that the strike will not defeat itself. The police are left on duty, so that disorder will not take place and the Government be furnished a reason for calling in troops. Milk wagons and restaurants are permitted to operate, so that people may be fed. Movies are allowed to go on, to keep the rank and file contented and out of mischief. But, with every such exemption, the strikers weaken the effect of their sudden blow. The proprietors of industry will certainly not surrender their property except in a cataclysm. The ordinary strike is merely a bargaining weapon: the employers consent to an agreement in order to avoid further loss and inconvenience. But no employer can be expected to surrender his all for any such reason. There is no half-way ground between violent revolution and the sort of strike which aims at ultimate conciliation.

This being the case the Canadian leaders used the worst possible tactics. If they were not aiming at revolution, they made a grave mistake in prefacing their effort by utterances which gave the employers and the public cause to fear it. If – as is highly improbable – they were aiming at revolution, they were singularly naive to suppose it could be effected without popular support and the use of superior force. Their objects should have been carefully defined, and their means adapted to their ends. They might have made a strong plea for industrial unionism and the kind of collective bargaining they wished, on the ground that it is essential, under modern conditions, for the protection of the employee.

They might, if political results were aimed at, have said so frankly and arranged a short strike as a demonstration. But to embark on a more or less general strike for uncertain objects and an indefinite period is to lunge blindly into the dark.

The Canadian unionists might learn wisdom from their comrades in the mother country. There the strongest and most effective organizations regard the strike as the very last resort. They take care to build up their case thoroughly and to air it extensively in public before acting. Months ago what would have been very like a general strike was projected by the British miners, railway men, and transport workers. The object was almost revolutionary – the nationalization of the mines and railways. Never for a moment has the British Government been allowed to forget the imminence of such a strike. But the strike has not been called. The leaders have turned the pressure into political channels; they have a good case, they are not afraid of argument, and they prefer to win by persuasion. The threat of a strike is merely used to set going discussion and official action. Men like Robert Smillie and J. H. Thomas know that destructive and hampering forces alone can never build the new world they desire.

---

11 THE STRIKE WAS WRONG

*The Grain Growers' Guide, Winnipeg
July 2, 1919*

BIG STRIKE ENDED

On June 26, the great general strike in Winnipeg collapsed, in utter and complete failure. The Strike Committee, realizing that all possibility of success had faded away, officially called off the strike without securing any of the demands for which the strike was called. No explanation, nor public statement, was made by the Strike Committee, and the workers on strike were simply instructed to go back to work. There immediately ensued a great rush for the jobs which they vacated six weeks before. The great majority found their jobs still vacant, but hundreds found their positions filled, and were not reinstated. A large number of returned soldiers were taken on at the post office, city hall, and by private employers to fill the vacancies created by the strikers, and their positions were made permanent. Immediately following the notice that the strike was off the city began to resume its normal activity, and within a few days practically all business was being carried on as usual.

The general strike in Winnipeg was the first of its kind in Canada. A few radical leaders, taking advantage of the general unrest, due to the high cost of living, succeeded in calling 35,000 men and women from their work. These leaders attempted to set up an autocratic government in Winnipeg and coerce the community by starvation. By alluring promises, held out to the striking unions, they succeeded in maintaining their support week after week. The strikers lost in wages, probably not far short of $1,000,000 per week. Gradually, as the rosy promises of the Strike Committee failed to materialize, the workers lost confidence in their leaders, and the strike began to disintegrate. By tens, and soon by hundreds, the strikers began to go back to work, and the Strike Committee realized, all too late, that its control over the unions had ceased, and that its designs to establish a new system of government was [sic] a complete and disastrous failure.

The failure of the general strike in Winnipeg is by no means to be considered as a condemnation of organized labor. Trades unionism has suffered a setback, but will recover, and should recover its entire strength. Trade unionism, properly conducted, is one of the greatest bulwarks of civilization, and the most powerful curb upon the rapacity of financial and industrial interests. But trades unionism can only make permanent progress when wisely led and when its demands are in accord with the very best interests of the community at large. The Winnipeg strike failed completely because it was wrong. Many of its leaders preached the worst doctrines of Bolshevism, confiscation and rule by force. They attempted to lead the strikers to believe that they were entitled to confiscate the wealth of the community for their own use, and that only those in the trades unions were entitled to a return for their labor. The propaganda put out by some of the strike leaders undoubtedly had its effect upon a considerable number of the strikers. But today, they are disillusioned. They realize that no community can exist except through co-operation. They realize that the existing order of things cannot be overturned in a day by exercise of force, and the great bulk of organized labor has no desire to overturn our constitutional form of government.

The Winnipeg strike failed because it was wrong. It was because the strike was wrong that all the big international unions refused to sanction it, and the big railway organizations declined to go on strike in sympathy. When challenged with starvation or submission, ten thousand or more of the non-union citizens of Winnipeg, men and women, manned the public utilities and the industries providing the necessities of life. They demonstrated that the city could not be starved by the refusal of organized labor to carry on. The demonstration afforded by non-union citizens was a striking object lesson to the strike leaders, and will undoubtedly prevent a recurrence of a general strike in any city in Canada.

When peaceful means failed to accomplish the purpose of the strike, violence was resorted to on the part of some, but the forces of law and order were more powerful and demonstrated that nothing but peaceful methods would be permitted. Had mob violence been allowed to prevail the community would shortly have been in a state of anarchy. A number of strike leaders are under arrest awaiting trial, which will take place according to the due process of the law. In the meantime, the workers of Winnipeg have nearly all returned to their former occupations. They will undoubtedly turn their attention henceforth more to the ballot than to the strike as a method of securing needed reforms. In this direction they are following constitutional methods and will be able to accomplish more than could be accomplished by the methods of the general strike. A Royal Commission will be appointed to investigate the causes of the strike and to bring in recommendations as to improving conditions which led to the strike. It is probably well that the plans of radical labor leaders have been tried and failed, even though the general strike was a costly disaster. The effect of the failure will have a powerful influence upon the community at large and will direct the efforts of organized labor into legitimate channels.

12 THERE IS GREATER WORK TO DO

The Telegram, Winnipeg
June 19, 1919

Now that the general strike is dying a natural and quiet death, there may be a tendency develop on the part of those citizens who organized themselves in defence of our democracy to lose interest in their splendid work, to regard it as completed, and to disintegrate as organizations.

Every one is weary, every one is overwrought, every one's nerves are ragged. This is a condition that invites disintegration. This fact ought to be recognized, and steps ought to be taken to combat it.

No more useful, no more patriotic association of citizens was ever brought into existence in Canada than the so-called Citizens' Committee of One Thousand – which might much more properly be called the Committee of all Good Citizens.

It was due largely to its efforts that Winnipeg was able to carry on in the darkest days of attempted revolution. It was due very largely to its efforts that the splendid volunteer army was made available for the preservation of law and order and for the upholding of the constitution. It was due largely to its efforts that the special police were made available in such numbers. It was solely due to the fact that the Citizens' Committee, from its inception, stood not for one class and not for one interest but for all the loyal people that it was able to rally to its standard these patriotic men and women who endured sacrifices that may never properly be appreciated, for the prevention of a general paralysis here that would have been fatal. Had the Citizens' Committee not stood for the high and unselfish principles for which it did stand, it could never have obtained the means necessary or the personal support necessary to enable it to accomplish its purpose.

The Citizens' Committee is more directly representative of the people of Winnipeg than is any administrative body that we have in this City or this Province. Such an organization, with capacity for so much good – a capacity that has been overwhelmingly demonstrated – must not be permitted to disintegrate. It must be perpetuated, if we are not to blind ourselves to the lessons of the past weeks and to permit indifference to deprive us of the opportunity for advancement along civic, provincial and federal economic lines such as may not recur in another generation.

If the Citizens' Committee were, as the revolutionaries would have us believe, merely an organization of capitalistic employers, it could not survive the end of the strike. Indeed, it would have lapsed into impotency long since. If it were merely an organization of any one class, representing any special interest, it would have been doomed to failure from its inception. Representing, as it does, all loyal classes, working for no selfish purpose, advancing no private interest, but concentrating its efforts and making its sacrifices solely for the general public good, it has become and has revealed itself as a body possessing the capacity and the will of an exalted type of communistic association.

The termination of the present strike will not remove the basic causes of that strike without effort. The economic conditions that made thousands of good citizens the easy victims of the duplicity of a handful of scheming charlatans still exist. Those conditions must be removed. We cannot depend upon our political parties or our governments of any variety or stripe to change those conditions to our satisfaction, or to make the soil of this country so fatal to the seeds of Bolshevism that our institutions will be secured.

We must depend upon ourselves, depend upon our own civic spirit, depend upon our own intelligence, to keep us organized to work in the public good, irrespective of former economic views, former prejudices and former habits of mind and association.

Such a body as the Citizens' Committee, established as a permanent institution, can exert an enormous pressure upon our constituted authorities to compel such redresses of real grievances as will remove discontent and cause the honest working man to turn from the revolutionary agitator with a smile of incredulity and disgust.

The Federal authorities must be forced by the weight of organized intelligence and soundly loyal public opinion to bring the cost of living down to a level where men and women can live without discouragement and enjoy the fruits of their labor without dividing them with an adventurous exploiter.

Perhaps this is too big a job for the Citizens' Committee of one city to accomplish. But the example of the Citizens' Committee of Winnipeg will assuredly be followed by the citizens of other cities and then the organized intelligence of all our great communities can act as a unit so powerful that it will be irresistible.

In the Provincial field the same opportunity will be furnished for bringing about a redress of real grievances, an improvement in economic methods that will directly and indirectly make for the happiness of the people.

In the civic field there is also an enormous opportunity for invaluable work. Our system of municipal government must be radically reformed. Inefficiency must be eradicated. It cannot be eradicated without eradicating the system that invites and encourages inefficiency.

The business of Winnipeg is the business of every citizen. The citizens must see in the future that their affairs must be placed in the most competent hands available – hands that are not tied by red tape, that are not paralyzed by obsolete machinery and that are not directed by any one class to the injury of any other class. In any circumstances, such a disgraceful and humiliating spectacle as we now suffer in Winnipeg municipal affairs must never again be furnished – where two of our sworn representatives, two of our city aldermen, are locked up in Stony Mountain on a charge of conspiracy against the King, conspiracy against the State, conspiracy against the very people whose sworn protectors they are.

Hold the Citizens' Committee together by all means; hold the patriotic men who have undergone more than a month of inconvenience, loss and hardship in our volunteer army – hold them as members of a greatly enlarged Citizens' Committee; encourage every other good and law-abiding citizen to join up in this community organization – and we shall have the machinery that will enable us to accomplish a work that will be of such enduring benefit that we shall look back a short time hence to the great Winnipeg general strike and its revolutionary attempt as a blessing in disguise – a blessing that not only we but our descendants will enjoy.

---

13 SOLIDARITY FOREVER

The One Big Union Monthly, Chicago July, 1919

The General Strike In Canada

The industrial unionists of Canada, the champions of the "One Big Union" have been forced into the necessity of testing their strength through a general strike of the larger part of the country.

The ostensible cause of the strike was the demand of the workers in the metal trades' for increased pay and for collective bargaining in the city of Winnipeg. This strike started on May 15th.

In a brief time it was found necessary to call out all the workers of Winnipeg in support of the strikers.

This was done so succcessfully [sic] that the strike committee was in complete control of the city, even the police and the municipal employees joining the strikers.

The employers, backed by a government hostile to the One Big Union movement refused to back down. It was plain from the start that the affair was something more than a common scrap over small differences between workers and their employers.

Everybody feels and knows that it is a general muster of the two opposing world forces of today preparatory to the final battle.

The strike soon spread westward and eastward until practically the whole country is [sic] shut down. The railroad employees are now considering the question of joining the strike.

There is a show of working class solidarity hardly ever equalled, a sign of the times that promises well for the future.

The strike is better understood when seen against the background of capitalist oppression and exploitation. Never before has the capitalist class of any country become more shamelessly reckless than the Canadian capitalists at the present time. It looks as if they gathered all their forces to break the workers down and kill their aspirations. The cost of living was driven up altogether out of proportion to the wages, free speech, free press and free assemblage were abolished, and the powers that be rode roughshod over the workers, much as they are doing here.

This explains the ready response of the workers to the strike call.

The original issue has become entirely submerged under the bigger question of which class shall rule society in the future, and the workers are in this manner having their thought molded in the forms of the future.

Every strike must end some day – in victory – in defeat or in compromise!

Victory in the present case would consist in the taking over of the industries by the workers through their industrial unions. Shall the present situation develop along those lines? That is a question which we will not undertake to answer.

The failure of the A. F. of L. to support the movement would tend to minimize such chances.

But no matter how it ends, the strike will be a great gain. It is to the workers what military training and organization is to the soldiers. The workers will come out of it with a schooling and a training which makes them twice as fit for the big battle of the future.

All hail to our brave Fellow Workers of Canada.

Guide to Journals

The Albertan, Calgary

Generally an independent paper politically, but conducted a vigorous rivalry with the *Calgary Herald*. It showed some sympathy with the strikers, but mainly used the situation to embarrass the federal government.

The Calgary Herald

Began as a daily in 1883. It was strongly Tory in sympathy and especially vituperative on the alien question.

The Guardian, Charlottetown

Founded in the early 1870's as a religious journal, it later became an influential and independent journal under J. E. B. McCready.

The Bulletin, Edmonton

Associated in its early years with Frank Oliver, Liberal Minister of the Interior in Laurier's cabinet. During the strike, it criticized the federal government but was also strongly opposed to the strikers.

The Globe, Toronto

Probably the most balanced account of the strike of all major newspapers. It opposed the principle of the general strike, yet sympathized with the workers and objected to the manner in which the federal government intervened.

The Manitoba Free Press, Winnipeg

Owned by Clifford Sifton and edited by John W. Dafoe during the strike. Dafoe was flatly opposed to the general strike as such but more sympathetic toward labour generally than the other Winnipeg dailies.

The Gazette, Montreal

The leading English-language, Tory paper in Montreal. Its attitude reflected

	business opinion closely. It was violently opposed to the strike and unsympathetic to the cause of unionism in general.
The Star, Montreal	Liberal organ in Montreal. It saw the strike in simplistic terms as a confrontation of Bolshevism and Democracy.
The Leader, Regina	Very stridently opposed to the strike, seeing it in terms of a Bolshevik conspiracy which threatened to engulf all of Western Canada.
The Post, Regina	Concentrated on the class aspect of the confrontation in Winnipeg. It tended to draw parallels between the One Big Union and American radical labor groups.
The Star, Toronto	One of the few major Canadian dailies which sympathized with labour while decrying extreme tactics. Unlike other papers, it pointed out that extremism was not a monopoly of labour.
The Times, Toronto	Consistently Red-baiting in its attitude and especailly vitriolic toward "aliens."
The Sun, Vancouver	Unique among metropolitan dailies as it consistently supported the strikers and condemned the actions of employers and the government.
The World, Vancouver	Attempted to be relatively impartial in its editorial policy but opposed a general strike in principle.
Western Labour News, Winnipeg	The organ of Western Canadian labour. It tended toward exaggerated class rhetoric preceding the strike but moderated its tone shortly after the strike began. Its editor, William Ivens, was arrested with the other strike leaders.

The Winnipeg Citizen	Founded by the Citizens' Committee of 1000. It claimed to be impartial in the original dispute but its avowed aim was to break the general strike. It resorted to quite reprehensible tactics in pandering to ethnic prejudice.
The Telegram, Winnipeg	The most bitter of the Winnipeg dailies against the strike. It was especially violent on the "alien" question.
The Tribune, Winnipeg	Attempted to be impartial on the economic issues of the strike. It ranged itself solidly against labour, however, on the use of the general strike as a tactic.

For Further Reading

Bercuson, David J.   "The Winnipeg General Strike, Collective Bargaining and the One Big Union Issue," *Canadian Historical Review* (June, 1970), pp. 164-177.

Graham, Roger.   *Arthur Meighen, Volume I: The Door of Opportunity*. Toronto: Clarke, Irwin and Company, 1960.

Jackson, James A.   *A Centennial History of Manitoba*. Toronto: McClelland and Stewart, 1970.

Jamieson, Stuart M.   *Times of Trouble*. Ottawa: Privy Council Office, 1966.

Masters, D. C.   *The Winnipeg General Strike*. Toronto: University of Toronto Press, 1950.

McNaught, Kenneth.   *A Prophet in Politics, A Biography of J. S. Woodsworth*. Toronto: University of Toronto Press, 1959.

Morton, W. L.   *Manitoba: A History*. Toronto: University of Toronto Press, revised edition, 1967.

Robin, Martin.   *Radical Politics and Canadian Labor, 1880-1930*. Kingston: Queen's University, 1968.

Royal Commission to Enquire Into and Report Upon the Causes and Effects of the General Strike Which Recently Existed in the City of Winnipeg For a Period of Six Weeks, Including the Methods of Calling and Carrying on Such Strike. Report of H. A. Robson K. C., Commissioner, Winnipeg, 1919.